MOMENTUM
Ready, Set, Go
How to move forward into your Destiny

APOSTLE GREGORY MCCURRY

Copyright © 2019 by Gregory McCurry
All rights reserved. This book or any portion thereof may not be reproduced or used in any manner whatsoever without the express written permission of the publisher except for the use of brief quotations in a book review.

Printed in the United States of America

First Printing, 2019

ISBN 978-1-7338770-2-2 (sc)
ISBN 978-1-7338770-3-9 (e)

McCurry Ministries International
2060 West 65th Street
Cleveland, Ohio 44102
(216) 916-9270

www.MyNewBeginning.org

MOMENTUM
Ready, Set, Go
How to move forward into your Destiny

Foreword

Have you ever tasted something and all of a sudden, your senses begin to come to life? Well, get ready to enjoy one of the best adventures of your life. As you digest this awesome, fresh and insightful look at this statement of Love – MOMENTUM – "The amount of force a moving body has because of its weight and the speed at which it is moving."

Momentum works the same no matter who you are. If, for example, you take a big rock, it will not travel very fast until you give it a push on a downhill slope. THEN YOU WATCH OUT as the momentum in it makes it move. Momentum is a moving force that overcomes resistance. 1 John 2:5-6 says, "But whoever keeps His word, truly the love of God is perfected in him. By this we know that we are in Him. He who says he abides in Him ought himself also to walk just as He walked."

Momentum is simply the force or speed of movement that carries an object to its final destination. If you want to BREAKTHROUGH, you need to have a certain amount of momentum housed in you. In order for a rocket to blast into space, it needs tremendous momentum to break the gravitational barrier - but with the enormous power of jet engines and rocket fuel, the ship is propelled faster, and faster until it breaks free of the earth's gravitational pull.

To my son, Greg, the writer of this anointed book, "Your best has just begun". I Decree and declare you are in full Momentum. I love you.

Dad and Chief
Apostle Leon D. Nelson

Acknowledgements

I want to first thank my wife, my partner in life and Ministry, my best friend Teresa S. McCurry. I LOVE YOU to ETERNITY, you have Inspired so many people, But THANK YOU for Inspiring Me!! Be Blessed forever.

I must say I really appreciate my wife, she inspired me to writing a book and it was way harder than I thought, and more rewarding than I could have ever imagined. None of this would have been possible without Kenneth Ndlovu, My content editor. Secondly, my Spiritual father Chief-Apostle Leon D. Nelson. He stood by me during every struggle and all my successes. That is a true spiritual father and friend.

I'm eternally grateful to him and his wife Pastor Margie Nelson. My parents Herbert B. McCurry (deceased) & Hattie E. McCurry who taught me discipline, tough love, manners, respect, and so much more that has helped me succeed in life. I truly have no idea where I'd be if it hadn't been for their love and guidance. My Children Greg Jr, Nichelle (Damion) Daniels, Michael, Sonja Jr, Deborah you all kept a brother on his knees. My Brother James E. McCurry (Maxine), My nieces Dawn & Denise, My Sister Sondra D. McCurry – it is because of their efforts and encouragement that I have a legacy to pass on to my family where one didn't exist before

TESTIMONIALS

TESTIMONIAL 01: Matt Johnson – 1

TESTIMONIAL 02: Belinda Grogan – 8

TESTIMONIAL 03: Teresa S. McCurry (Pastor Tee) – 18

TESTIMONIAL 04: Sis Olymithia Freeman – 23

TESTIMONIAL 05: Ms. Delicia Mayes R.T. (R)(MR) – 32

TESTIMONIAL 06: Dr. Jonathan J. Pullin – 37

TESTIMONIAL 07: Elder Kimberly Moss PhD – 43

TESTIMONIAL 08: Sis Annette Worwell – 55

TESTIMONIAL 09: Terrie Sylvester – 58

TESTIMONIAL 10: Pastor Adreane Russell – 63

TESTIMONIAL 11: Deacon Willis McNeal – 67

TESTIMONIAL 12: Rosetta Gloster – 71

TESTIMONIAL 13: Evangelist Mattie Daniels-McNeal – 75

TESTIMONIAL 14: Bishop Charles & Pastor Carmen Dorsey – 80

TESTIMONIAL 15: Godfrey Tull – 87

TESTIMONIAL 16: Janet Tull – 89

TESTIMONIAL 17: Richanda Jackson – 95

TESTIMONIAL 18: Elder Natasha Williams – 99

TESTIMONIAL 19: Pastor Brian Timberlake – 104

TESTIMONIAL 20: Pastor Antoine Burts – 108

TESTIMONIAL 21: Pastor Denise Washington – 114

TESTIMONIAL 22: Lenora Flecher – 118

CONTENTS

Foreword v

Acknowledgements VII

- CHAPTER 01: The Year Of The Momentum 1
- CHAPTER 02: Expectation Of The Momentum 19
- CHAPTER 03: The Movement of Momentum 37
- CHAPTER 04: The Momentum of Faith 55
- CHAPTER 05: The Sound Of The Momentum 73
- CHAPTER 06: Momentum – Something Out Of Nothing 97
- CHAPTER 07: To The Great Years Of Momentum Ahead............ 107

List of appendices 120

About the Author 121

CHAPTER 1

The Year Of The Momentum

> **Testimonial**
>
> I would like to sum up Apostle Greg McCurry using these four words, as it relates to the impact that he has had on, and in my life.
> He is: (1) Consistent, and (2) Genuine. (3) He has much Wisdom, and (4) Provides Protection to all of us against our spiritual vulnerabilities.
> I have given him a place in my life as spiritual father for some years now, but the connection extends beyond spiritual matters. This is also someone I can crack jokes and laugh together with, sit down over dinner, talk about sports and fitness, etc. Never at once have I overstepped my boundaries when I am, or not with him, as long as it concerns him, rather I've always held and will always hold him in high esteem and honor, as my spiritual father.
>
> ~ Matt Johnson

I came into this year by no luck, but I fully made it here, and operating in, and by the blessing of God. I did not barely make it, but I made it on full-strength – all in God's Grace and mercy.

Life is what you make it, and what you make it comes out of how strong you (make) yourself feel. I say this on purpose, that you are the one that actually makes yourself feel strong, because this all goes down to the kind of attitude that you show to life, and eventually God, to whom you should look up to for everything that you do.

Therefore, when I say that I did not barely make it into this year, this is me declaring that I have been so blessed in the past year, and that I have been given much strength, beyond measure, to launch myself into this year on a much stronger ground than before. This is just me proclaiming that I have been able to build the kind of momentum that I need in order for me to perform like a well-oiled machine in this year. And I know that once I proclaim such, my body is readied for the kind of work that I know needs to be put into all the programs of the year ahead.

Planning ahead don't just take writing notes down, but is a process that should involve everything that you got, and will potentially have in the future. Therefore, this also requires a buy-in from your body itself – for the right body language throughout. When I say that this is going to be the year of the momentum, I do not believe I just say it from my mouth, without a positive body language to accompany the statement, neither do I expect the same from you.

> **Proverbs 29:18 /KJV/**
> *Where there is no vision, the people perish: but he that keepeth the law, happy is he.*

Now, we spoke of proclaiming the year ahead as that of momentum, and also about how much your body has to show the zeal to partake in it (momentum). When all is said and done, it all boils down to vision – that you ought to provide the vision for yourself, because the lack of it leads to destruction. It does not matter that we could have provided the vision for the year here in church, the most important point of the matter is that you ought to carry that to your home, to your workplace, simply because that is where you live your life on a daily basis, and Christianity, our faith in God, is a lifestyle; you live it every day.

Now I want to take a look at a few definitions before delving more into the chapter.

Momentum

The word itself resonates very well with Physics, not that I am a lover of science, but I guess this is something where we can start from. However, I believe that we exist because of God, and that God created science around us, not that we exist because scientific movements happened some millions of years ago, again, this is just saying, and I guess this is the point where you can let out a little smile with me.

Now to the definition of momentum according to Physics, it speaks of the amount of movement that an object possesses. When speaking of momentum, this is not just movement in mere terms, but it is movement that can be seen and felt so much so that even if the object is still moving, it still has more movement that is housed in it so that it will not be easy to stop it from moving.

Thus, momentum in Physics equals the mass times the velocity of an object, meaning that the momentum of an object is directly proportional to the amount of the mass of an object and its velocity, the key feature here being the mass. Now, let me remind you again, I said that I came into this year on full-force, meaning that inside of me, I believe that I have gathered enough mass to take me to great momentum that is enough to launch an awesome life for me. This is to say that even if we are coming from the previous years, we have been building the mass inside of our bodies and we will mention this part further in the book. Just remember that this mass is still in you even if you have taken off and will determine how far you are going to go.

This is more about running the race and winning. And the focus when running is not just on being able to successfully take off, but to keep the speed going, to keep the acceleration on, and to be able to outrun all the obstacles. You can only do this of you have gathered enough momentum in you.

According to the above, my interest now becomes that part where it mentions the amount of motion that will still be housed in an object that is still moving. I will once again mention that I did not barely make it into 2019, but I made it on full-force, knowing that I am on the move and that nothing will stop the kind of motion that I still possess in me. This is the kind of motion that is enough to see me through the year, and I can confess that by the time we end the year 2019, I will still be running just because God has built enough momentum in me, and I was a willing participant.

Therefore, in a Christian's perspective, I want to coin the definition of momentum as the outcome of the force on which a believer takes off, in the Christian race, combined with the amount of faith that one has gathered before the race began.

To dig a little into my definition, Faith is a powerful ingredient and it represents the mass that an object (a believer) has in him or her. This makes what will carry you through the race and will make sure that you do not stop moving. The level of take-off with which you make is then the velocity, or the speed that is going to determine how much you are still going to fare throughout the race. As a Christian, you ought to understand that there are as many things to be met along the way, many challenges, many obstacles and many naysayers that will require your full-velocity to make sure that when they try to apply brakes on you, the result is you keep on going. You also ought to carry a huge mass in you (that of faith) and be like a fully loaded dump truck that is always difficult to apply brakes on, just because it has so much mass (Faith) in it pushing it through.

For this part, we will feature the verses that come from the book of Joshua chapter three. I pray that you read this out aloud before diving into what I will write about it soon after.

> **Joshua 3:1-17 / NIV /**
> *1 Early in the morning Joshua and all the Israelites set out from Shittim and went to the Jordan, where they camped before crossing over. 2 After three days the officers went throughout the camp,*

3 giving orders to the people: "When you see the ark of the covenant of the LORD your God, and the Levitical priests carrying it, you are to move out from your positions and follow it. 4 Then you will know which way to go, since you have never been this way before. But keep a distance of about two thousand cubits between you and the ark; do not go near it." 5 Joshua told the people, "Consecrate yourselves, for tomorrow the LORD will do amazing things among you." 6 Joshua said to the priests, "Take up the ark of the covenant and pass on ahead of the people." So they took it up and went ahead of them. 7 And the LORD said to Joshua, "Today I will begin to exalt you in the eyes of all Israel, so they may know that I am with you as I was with Moses. 8 Tell the priests who carry the ark of the covenant: 'When you reach the edge of the Jordan's waters, go and stand in the river.' " 9 Joshua said to the Israelites, "Come here and listen to the words of the LORD your God. 10 This is how you will know that the living God is among you and that he will certainly drive out before you the Canaanites, Hittites, Hivites, Perizzites, Girgashites, Amorites and Jebusites. 11 See, the ark of the covenant of the Lord of all the earth will go into the Jordan ahead of you. 12 Now then, choose twelve men from the tribes of Israel, one from each tribe. 13 And as soon as the priests who carry the ark of the LORD—the Lord of all the earth—set foot in the Jordan, its waters flowing downstream will be cut off and stand up in a heap." 14 So when the people broke camp to cross the Jordan, the priests carrying the ark of the covenant went ahead of them. 15 Now the Jordan is at flood stage all during harvest. Yet as soon as the priests who carried the ark reached the Jordan and their feet touched the water's edge, 16 the water from upstream stopped flowing. It piled up in a heap a great distance away, at a town called Adam in the vicinity of Zarethan, while the water flowing down to the Sea of the Arabah (that is, the Dead Sea) was completely cut off. So the people crossed over opposite Jericho. 17 The priests who carried the ark of the covenant of the LORD stopped in the middle of the Jordan and stood on dry ground, while all Israel passed by until the whole nation had completed the crossing on dry ground.

From reading the verses above, there are some key factors to take home: First is that fact that the Israelites were on the move, they had already gathered some momentum in them. Just a post script on this one, *Israelites had to take forty years in the wilderness instead of a mere few weeks as according to God's plan because their momentum had died along the way as one key ingredient that we spoke about had depleted in them – FAITH, they had lost all faith in God and were always complaining and doubting His intentions of taking them out of the land of Egypt.*

Second is the fact that the Israelites were moving together, and were one as a group, thus God was always present in them. We see in a number of verses where it says 'God said to Joshua...' in a clear sign that He was always with them. The Israelites were always united, even in complaining against God!

Now that God was amongst them and that they were on the move, the bearers of the Ark of God stepped ahead and when they got their feet into the shores of the river Jordan, the water that was coming from upstream stood in a huge heap so that there could be dry ground for the Israelites to step on.

Testimonial

Apostle Greg McCurry has been such a Blessing to me. He has encouraged me when my faith was challenged through sickness and in need of a procedure that was to be done. He reminded me it was already done in the name of Jesus! God has truly anointed him to the position that he is in, in order to tell the world about the Lord Jesus Christ. I can go on and on about the love that he shows and the friendship that he shares so freely. Much love and many Blessings Apostle Greg McCurry.

~ Belinda Grogan.

FAITTH was at work! God told them beforehand what He was going to do with the water in the river Jordan and they believed, it so happened and they walked on dry ground and to the other side! Now, we go back to that part where I spoke of the many obstacles that may stand in your way as you will be moving in this Christian life, that was one hell of an obstacle that the Israelites were facing, yet because they believed in God's promise to separate the waters in the river Jordan, they walked through their obstacle as if nothing was standing before them. With enough momentum (that is mass which is faith and proper take off which is velocity) no obstacle is enough to stop you from getting to the other side with a smile plastered all over your face.

Momentum works well with Confidence

In the Bible, we learn of King David during his youthful days when he came face to face with Goliath the giant. So many interesting things happened in the build-up to the face-off, until the time when he stood in front of the Philistine. As many things happened, one observation stood out of the rest – the fact that David as a young boy was very confident of what he could do using whatever was at his disposal. He just had great faith in his ability.

We want to go to the issue of naysayers when in the race of life.

> **1 Samuel 17:32-37 / NIV /**
>
> *32 David said to Saul, "Let no one lose heart on account of this Philistine; your servant will go and fight him." 33 Saul replied, "You are not able to go out against this Philistine and fight him; you are only a young man, and he has been a warrior from his youth." 34 But David said to Saul, "Your servant has been keeping his father's sheep. When a lion or a bear came and carried off a sheep from the flock, 35 I went after it, struck it and rescued the sheep from its mouth. When it turned on me, I seized it by its hair, struck it and killed it. 36 Your servant has killed both the lion and the bear; this uncircumcised Philistine will be like one of them, because he has defied the armies of the living God. 37 The LORD who rescued me from the paw of the lion and the paw of the bear will rescue me from the hand of this Philistine." Saul said to David, "Go, and the LORD be with you."*

In verse 32 of the above, David, as a young boy, offered to face Goliath in battle for he had great faith in his abilities. Momentum, remember in our Christian world we have said that is a combination of your FAITH and the great pace with which you take off in the race of life. However, even if David had such belief, I can imagine him speaking with great authority, that 'I can face and defeat this man who is busy showing off in front of God's chosen people,' still King Saul found reason to throw doubt in front of the young man's path. I can imagine if your pastor, father or any senior person in your life comes to you and says you cannot do anything at all and that you are not fit just for completing a single task? Many of us would believe that and say need to go back to the drawing board and get things in order! Now imagine David having to hear this not from anyone but the king himself?

Even if all this happened to David, we ought to know that naysayers are everywhere and this can happen to you whilst you are relaxed with the people that you trust the most. What to do when these people speak is what David's response was from verse 34, starting by reminding Saul what he has been doing.

"Your servant has been keeping his father's sheep…" Those were part of the opening words for his response. Effective, positive momentum works well where someone has already been doing something. Here, David mentions first that he has been keeping his father's sheep, and before going all the way to how he protected the sheep you know that here is someone who has already been busy. Always remind your naysayers that you have been working on something meaning that you can still do more, and so you will be able to do so. Yes, this is something that you can positively say, well, unless if you had been doing nothing at all, then when some are on stage two, you would be still struggling to get hold of the terms of the first stage!

I say this in order to take you back to the part where I did mention that we indeed have been moving in the past year, and that whatever we have been doing during this part brought us to this day and thus this same year. Things do not just happen in a Christian's life, but there has to be a history of well worked out tasks, duties and responsibilities. You ought to do these full of gratitude to God.

> **Colossians 3:23 / NIV /**
> *Whatever you do, work at it with all your heart,*
> *as working for the Lord, not for human masters*

Now moving along with young David's response, he then goes on to mention that not only did he tend his father's sheep, but the sheep had from time to time been getting into trouble with not only just wild animals, but lions and bears. David told the king how much he had been able to defeat the beasts and then finishes off his response by presenting himself as superior than his enemy when he referred to Goliath as "this Philistine."

As soon as you take record of what you have been doing, and then positively put yourself above the challenge, then you would have greatly built a positive momentum around yourself. Because David did well all the above, this whole story culminated in the giant Philistine lying face down from just a small stone from a little boy's sling, defeated [1 Samuel 17:49]. The stone had so much momentum that is sunk in the head of the Philistine, it could not just stop outside his forehead, because it could not be stopped. Good momentum should not be easy to stop.

Vision

We have spoken at great length about the word momentum, which makes sense as it makes the subject of this entire book. However, it is also quite imperative to understand terms such as vision and others to follow in line with what this book has to achieve.

Having been around for some time in this life, I have realised that life is made up of billions of people around the earth, yet there are just a few visionaries.

Inasmuch as this may be true, we ought to understand this important piece of information, that even if we know that there are a few visionaries in life, the fact of the matter is all of us have to carry some sort of a vision about our lives. This is simply because we are moving from wherever we are today to some place that we should be tomorrow, how you are going to get there is a mystery, which is where vision comes into play – you ought to premeditate, and plan out your course of movement tomorrow, today. You do this, you surely will live a BLESSED life.

> **Proverbs 29:18 / KJV /**
> *Where there is no vision, the people perish: but he that keepeth the law, happy is he.*

Going into the online English dictionary, a vision is (1) the faculty or state of being able to see, or (2) the ability to think about or plan the future with imagination or wisdom.

The first definition needs no more explanation as it speaks

directly to literally being able to see, something that everyone understands and knows that all the people with no eye sight problems have this kind of vision. In other words, only the naturally blind do not possess this kind of a vision, meaning that it does not require something special in order to possess it.

The second definition now becomes interesting, as it adds in words like the future, planning, thinking, imagination and wisdom. Now, this is the kind of vision that even the blind people can have, because it is a function that is applied through the mind and not just by the eyes. This is also the kind of vision that not everyone else can possess. However, even of it is difficult for everyone to be disciplined enough to have this kind of vision, we just ought to have it as it speaks of seeing into the future well in advance and then coming up with ways of making that future beautiful.

How does all this tie into momentum? Well, when gathering great momentum for running a race, you surely will not just be running a race for no reason at all, but you are in this race because you are envisioning a certain destination where you want to carry yourself into. Now, mapping out that destination beforehand requires someone with that kind of vision where the future is expertly thought about, as in the second definition of the word vision above.

Luck

Luck is when one happens to benefit from something that he or she does not deserve, or has not been working towards. It's sort of an unspoken rule that good Christians refrain from using the word "luck" when describing happy circumstances. By far the more spiritual word is "blessed," for it connotes divine intervention by God as opposed to mere chance. But when speaking of real things in life, we do not encourage people to sit down, fold their hands and hope to get lucky during the race of life.

We don't believe in luck we believe in God's grace in the form of BLESSINGS!! Everything that happens should be seeking God first for guidance and proper vision. God knows everything and can direct us from afar off and we can patiently works towards those. Therefore, indeed we did not get into this year by luck, and likewise, we are not looking to finish the year by luck, thus we are moving with people that are willing to gather as much momentum within themselves and be able to run this race for God. There is a BIG difference between thinking and saying I'm just lucky or believing I am blessed. It is your mind-set and heart of being one or the other. Being lucky is the idea that by chance, something in the universe made a situation go in your favour. Being blessed is acknowledgment in any given situation to the goodness of God. I am always in the mind-set of being BLESSED!!

> **James 1:7-8 (NKJV)**
> *7 For let not that man suppose that he will receive anything from the Lord; 8 he is a double-minded man, unstable in all his ways.*

Partake

The last that I am going to look into is to 'partake'. This is quite important for me here, as this word means to participate or join in an activity. Partake may also mean to eat or drink something according to the online English dictionary.

Why partake? Well, we are all a group of Christians that believe in God the Father, the Son and the Holy Spirit. We share the same belief and are looking to build this momentum together as believers. Well, in order for this to work well in this year, you ought to be able to participate fully in the work that we are going to be doing as a ministry, wherever you are. This is not the year to be waiting for the pastor to come and drag you out of your house for the midweek service, but you alone ought to be willing to participate in this cause. When things work out like this, then we can speak of greater things to look forward to in this year of the momentum.

***

Beloved ones, it delights me to have another opportunity to speak to the world through the writing of books, and this time, we are looking at what makes you move, what makes you go places in life – The Momentum. I understand we are saying that this year is the year of momentum, but remember also that life is all about continuity. After we build this momentum in this year, it is going to take us further to the next years of our lives. This therefore means that whatever that is we are doing now should be properly done, as unto the Lord and not unto men.

This is the first chapter of this book, and I hope it has

already given you an interesting perspective into the subject of momentum and how much you need this if you are to launch a great first step into just anything about your life. We are blessed that God blessed us with a lot of spiritual blessings, that we can use until and beyond a good life here on Earth, but we need to build enough momentum within in order to launch that great first step with FAITH, for the journey is quite long ahead. Always remember that momentum is that combination of the mass that you have in your body and the speed at which you are moving. We have likened the body mass to your faith which should always be great, and also likened the speed you move with to the take-off that you make in this Christian Journey.

Remember always to stay confident throughout the entire year in order to fully experience the momentum together with others. We would hate to see another Israelites situation where their journey to Canaan lasted for decades when it was just supposed to be a few weeks simply because they failed to maintain their momentum by having FAITH in God's promise.

Testimonial

Apostle Gregory and I were united in holy matrimony on 7/7/07 @ 7pm. The number seven is one of the most significant numbers to be found in the Bible, because it is the number of spiritual perfection & completion. There are so many things that I could testify about my husband, but I just want to say that he is an amazing, spirit-filed leader of God's people, he is so patient and so kind, not just with me, but with everyone that he comes in contact with. He genuinely LOVES people and wants to see the best out of them. My husband has helped me to become a better person, and is the one who encouraged me to walk BOLDLY into my calling and operate in the Spiritual Gifts that God has blessed me with. He is an awesome father, both natural and spiritual. I thank God for him daily. What a treasure that we have in an earthly vessel called "MY SWEETIE GREG". I love you to life and I am SO Proud of you.

~ Teresa S. McCurry (Pastor Tee)

CHAPTER 2

Expectation Of The Momentum

God needs you to have the momentum, expect it! I delivered this word (tittle for this chapter) in December of 2018, when we had already made it clear that the theme for the year 2019 was going to be Momentum. It was a perfect message to deliver, and get everyone expecting to make moves and be expectant on building momentum in the year 2019.

It was great indeed, to witness the kind of atmosphere when the message was being delivered.

We spoke of this year being that of the momentum, and we also mentioned how the whole momentum truth works in a Christian world, with FAITH being at the centre of it all. Moving ahead, I am speaking to you with regards to expecting the momentum, right in this moment! We are believers in Christ, and do believe that through the word of God, we will be able to greatly understand what this book is about and be able to build great momentum in our Christian lives, family lives, professional lives, as well as in our individual journeys. All this, we are able to comprehend because we are believers in the word of God.

Psalm 119:130 / KJV /
The entrance of thy words giveth light, it giveth understanding unto the simple.

According to the above scripture, all we need to gain as much understanding about the lessons of life and lessons about God and Christianity, like the one I am teaching through this book, is to let the words of God keep on entering into us. We do have the Bible for that purpose. Therefore, read on and gain as much understanding.

Every time you make a move towards a certain direction, you are making it in faith and in expectation of the momentum to move ahead in life. What begins at the start of any process is the expectation. Remember in the previous chapter I did write about the word vision. At this stage, I hope you understand that with vision, you are not expected to see what everyone sees, nor are you expected to believe in what is already built and can be physically felt. Vision, or being a visionary is being a game-changer is your sphere of influence. This is so because you see before others see, you feel before others feel, you build before anyone starts building and you are always ahead of the curve.

How does this all help in the expectation of the momentum? Well, momentum building has to be part of our daily lives simply because in life you move from place to place, you grow, you move around, even when in your house you move to the kitchen, to the living room, to the Bathroom and so forth. Failure to move will just result in you not having the luxury to enjoy a good cup of coffee from the kitchen and so forth. But here is the interesting thing now, that when making that move, you do so because you would have dreamt of sipping on that cup of coffee whilst busy reading in your study. So, because you would have thought of getting something nice for yourself and made a move, you would have acted on what you were envisioning.

Therefore, we build momentum so that we are able to have the motion towards the goals that we want to achieve in life, because it all involves movement.

The expectation of momentum is not something you can just tell me about, but this is something that I want to see, because when you have faith and are in expectation, you just start making moves and we do see that someone is moving.

When God created the heavens and the earth, the Bible says that the two realms were just one giant empty space with nothing on it (except for the water where the spirit of God was hovering over), and interestingly, the Spirit of God MOVED over this space. There was indeed movement back then and we all see and behold what came out of that! [Genesis 1:2]

After creating everything, God declared that it was good. Therefore, expect only the good from Him, and from the power of making a movement. In my Christian life, I have noticed that many are dormant Christian who just lie around for the whole year just coming to church a bit warm today, a bit cold tomorrow, and you do not even see that you are suffocating your own faith. There is no building of momentum when all you do is get cold for the rest of the year.

Revelation 3:15-16 / KJV /
15 I know thy works, that thou art neither cold nor hot: I would thy wet, cold or hot. 16 So then because thou art lukewarm, and neither cold nor hot, I will spue thee out of my mouth.

God is delighted when His people are well-defined in who they stand for, what they want to do and how much they are expecting from their Father. If you are to blow lukewarm and be not too sure of what you want from this church, then you might as well expect to be left behind when everyone gets going because they were expectant of the momentum and they worked on it until things started happening in their lives. This, what I am talking about here, is always the reason why most people are always looking around, wondering why so and so is always testifying of something that God would have done for them through the entire year, when you actually are wondering when is your turn coming next. The spirit of God sees, He is in our midst like all the time and He sees who is serious about their expectations and who is not.

I will tell you a typical example of people that get less-expectant when in church, these are those that get invited by a friend to church, and when they are here, the focus still remains on that friend, or they will still say they are doing it for the sake of their friend who invited them to church. Let me tell you something, in this journey, there are no groups of salvation, this is a journey of individuals that just gather together for the sake of encouraging each other in the Lord, yet when running the race, you got to put in the work yourself, and for yourself!

> **Testimonial**
>
> Since the beginning of the experience with Apostle Greg, he's taught me that faith makes all things possible, and that love makes all things easy, and lastly, he has shown me that hope makes all things work and most of all, GOD LOVES ME.
>
> ~ Sis Olymithia Freeman

On a particular day, you would also want to sit down, look back and rejoice for you would have made a really good account of yourself, before God and men.

> **2 Timothy 4:7-8 / NIV /**
> *7 I have fought the good fight, I have finished the race, I have kept the faith. 8 Now there is in store for me the crown of righteousness, which the Lord, the righteous Judge, will award to me on that day—and not only to me, but also to all who have longed for his appearing.*

Verse 7 closes off by saying, "I have kept the faith," and it makes a lot of sense, where we have already highlighted that momentum in a Christian's view is made up of an equation where momentum equals (FAITH + A GOOD TAKE-OFF). I can surely say that expecting the momentum when I am not moving in faith, when I have began the race very weak does not really put me in a good position to also partake when others are enjoying what God will have to bring to us.

We have made it to this far, there is no more turning back – that is the sound of expectation. I know that some of us have come through a lot of pain in 2018, but that does not have to take away your faith, nor should it take away your spiritual strength. Your spirit always has to be strong, and when I say I made it into 2019 on full-force, I should be able to say it even on a scared body, because my spirit believes, and it is strong enough to move me from place to place, it is strong enough to push me through the next phase of the journey, it is strong enough to help me build a strong refuge for myself in Christ. Here are a few Bible verses that reveal that the spirit indeed can be stronger that your flesh (body) and can carry you through in your journey of faith:

> **Matthew 26:41 / KJV /**
> *Watch and pray, that ye enter not into temptation: the spirit indeed is willing, but the flesh is WEAK.*

> **Romans 8:3 / KJV /**
> *For what the law could not do, in that it was WEAK through the FLESH, God sending His own Son in the likeness of sinful FLESH, and for sin, condemned sin in the FLESH.*

From reading above, you get to learn that indeed weakness starts in the flesh, and that kind of weakness will not really matter if the spirit is strong. When starting off in this race of faith, many could be feeling weak, inadequate or be stressed out about their private matters, well, in this place of worship, we lay aside every ounce of trouble and focus on making the spiritual being strong enough to propel us ahead. This is no place to mourn every day, this is no place to count your losses one-by-one, but this is a place of worship, where the spirit is made strong in order to balance the physical strength in the flesh also. When you rightly do this, then your spiritual equation of momentum works really well.

I also would want to hear you, in your time of weakness, shouting that you are strong, a confession that would make a world of a difference in the way that you are going to be running the race of life, today and forever.

> **Job 3:10 / KJV /**
> *Beat your plowshares into swords, and your pruning hooks into spears: Let the weak say I am strong*

In the above verse, God was preparing His people for war, and it was clear that one important aspect about life, which is farming, was now being sacrificed for war. This is revealed when He says they should beat their ploughshares into swords, and pruning hooks into spears. When in battle, it is always important to know and set your priorities right before making any single step. This beating of shares into swords, and pruning hooks into spears meant that the first thing that was now being made clear in everyone's mind was that we are now going for war, and no more turning back, everything else, even something as important as farming, was now being put into the second place. The war took first place and was supposed to be won at all costs. The last part now closes off by encouraging the weak to also proclaim that they are strong.

Why must the weak say I am strong?

This journey is a Christian one, and like we have mentioned before, it works in groups just as the Apostle Paul encouraged us to gather together from time to time so that we may encourage one another.

> **Hebrews 10:25 / KJV /**
> *Not forsaking the assembling of ourselves together, as the manner of some is; but exhorting one another: and so much more, as ye see the day approaching.*

When in this group, there are duties, which range from just encouraging one another, to protecting each other as well as looking after each other's many needs, just like Jesus Christ commanded us to love one another. Now, carrying out all these duties is truly not for the faint-hearted, but this is the work of mighty men in Christ, and how mighty you are in the Lord, or in faith is not really something we can measure using how big your body is, but we do this using how strong your spirit is, and this is something that you have to ignite yourself. It is not my duty as a church leader to make and keep you strong in spirit, but as a child of God, this is your responsibility to make sure that your spirit is in the right standing with God, and ready to start the momentum inside of you.

We indeed have duties to carry out in the name of Christ Jesus, and these all evolve around exhorting and protecting one another for the sake of the Kingdom of God. When we are all strong as a gathering, and have gathered great momentum in our individual lives, then it becomes easy for the vision of the church at large to grow exponentially, just because we would have all brought so much individual burning fires into the one big fire of God. You ought to understand that your weakness does not only bring you down as we will show just now, but it also brings down the whole congregation, so stay sharp and be encouraging to others.

Having said the above, I would like to outline just a few Bible scriptures that speak about Christians having to encourage one another.

> **Acts 14:22 / NIV /**
> *strengthening the disciples and encouraging them to remain true to the faith. "We must go through many hardships to enter the kingdom of God," they said.*

1 Thessalonians 4:1 / NIV /
As for other matters, brothers and sisters, we instructed you how to live in order to please God, as in fact you are living. Now we ask you and urge you in the Lord Jesus to do this more and more.

1 Timothy 2:1 / NIV /
I urge, then, first of all, that petitions, prayers, intercession and thanksgiving be made for all people

2 Tim 2:1-7 / NIV /
1 You then, my son, be strong in the grace that is in Christ Jesus. 2 And the things you have heard me say in the presence of many witnesses entrust to reliable people who will also be qualified to teach others. 3 Join with me in suffering, like a good soldier of Christ Jesus. 4 No one serving as a soldier gets entangled in civilian affairs, but rather tries to please his commanding officer. 5 Similarly, anyone who competes as an athlete does not receive the victor's crown except by competing according to the rules. 6 The hardworking farmer should be the first to receive a share of the crops. 7 Reflect on what I am saying, for the Lord will give you insight into all this.

From the verses that are outlined above, (Acts:22) encourages people to actually develop the culture of encouraging one another in the Lord, for we also believe that we can build momentum as individuals, hear the sound of it as individuals, but we can even do more when we encourage everyone that we have reach to, to remain in faith, create momentum, hear the sound of it and react to it in a magnificent way that is enough to bring so many blessings from above.

The other three parts of the above scripture (1 Thessalonians 4:1; 1 Timothy 2:1; 2 Timothy 2:1-7) speak of how a Christian can actually encourage another one. In all those cases, it was the Apostle Paul helping other to stay in the Lord, hence the main use of the word 'urge' in all those scriptures. Being in Christ really feels like a place where we just help each other do more in appreciating God and His presence (through the Holy Spirit) in our daily lives.

Now, having spoken much about how we have to stay encouraging one another, it becomes quite clear (of the need) to also mention the fact that some believers find it difficult to do things for Christ when they are weak in spirit. Therefore, the WEAK must say I am STRONG, and indeed stay strong so that in the end, we all hear, and react to the sound of the momentum, a perfect set-up to cultivate the ground for the blessings from God.

More so, the weak must also say that they are strong because in the end, we are supposed to be seen and heard fighting together as a group, hence the weak spots cannot not be a pleasant site in such scenarios. A group of fighters can only be as strong as its individual members.

Weak individuals in a group of fighters are a source of wasted resources that would have been channelled towards keeping their well-being. In the Christian movement, sometimes it might feel like it's OK to just come in and sit at the back, make sure that the pastor sees you, yet you do nothing to ignite the momentum. Do not even for a second think that you will be doing yourself a good service by acting all cunning, because in the end, there are both individual and group rewards, meaning that for the group reward, you may partake, but your individual rewards from God may be as disappointing, and even more so when these things shall be done in the open, where there will be nothing that is hidden from anyone.

The reasons above are why the Bible encourages others that are strong to encourage the weak in the Lord, because as a church, we would not be happy to in the end see a lot of inferior rewards for the others in the Kingdom of God when we were all here standing as soldiers in Christ.

> **Acts 20:35 / KJV /**
> *I have shewed you all things, how that so labouring ye ought to support the WEAK, and to remember the words of the Lord Jesus, how He said, it is more blessed to give than to receive.*

Romans 15:1 / KJV /
We then that are strong ought to bear the infirmities of the weak, and not to please ourselves.

There are however other exciting reasons why one should proclaim that they are strong when in their weaknesses. You can say I am strong when weak in order to enjoy life, no matter the circumstances, to rejoice even when weak.

2 Corinthians 12:9-19 / KJV /
And he said unto me, My grace is sufficient for thee: for my strength is made perfect in weakness. Most gladly therefore will I rather glory in my infirmities, that the power of Christ may rest upon me. 10 Therefore I take pleasure in infirmities, in reproaches, in necessities, in persecutions, in distresses for Christ's sake: For when I am WEAK, then I am STRONG.

***

Testimonial

My family recently experienced a scare moment (of almost losing my sister in August of 2018). My sister and I are very close, and at age 33, she had an abscess which sent her body into septic shock. She had to go under an emergency surgery that put her into a comma. The comma prompted her to be on a life support ventilation machine. When this happened, I called Apostle Gregory to have him pray for my sister.

He was very empathetic and had faith that she would pull through this tragic situation. I also started to get calls from members of the leadership and prayer team that they were praying for my sister and family too. That was heartwarming to me, the fact that he cared so much to involve a whole team of prayer warriors for us just after I had immediately informed him of this serious situation. I tried to keep myself busy so I wouldn't worry by working extra shifts and still attending church activities as normal but things were looking downhill.

Every time we got good news about her recovery something else would happen. Even though Apostle Gregory has a busy schedule, he took time out to check on how me and my family were handling things with my sister still on life support. Seeing your loved one in pain or going through something but can't help them takes a heavy toll on you, and doubt tries to creep in. Apostle Gregory constantly reminded me that everything will work out just fine because God will heal her and we already have the VICTORY through Jesus Christ!!! After two months, my sister finally woke up out of the comma, but was still on the ventilation machine. One Sunday after then church service, Apostle Gregory came to me and said, "We are getting your sister out of the ICU! What day can I come to the hospital to visit her with you?" I was so excited because I knew that I was about to see a move of God *(cont. next page)*

> The following day was a Monday (everyone in the church knows Mondays are his only day off so no contacting Apostle! Lol). However, I received a text message from him on his off day saying that he was confirming a visit with my sister for Tuesday. When Tuesday came, Apostle Gregory met me to visit my sister. He told her that he has faith that she will be out of ICU immediately! He stated that, "By His stripes you are healed." Then all three of us held hands together and agreed that she is healed in Jesus' name. Even though he didn't ask for it, my heart wanted to pay for his parking at the hospital. He did not want any money, he just enjoyed doing work for God's kingdom.
>
> That showed me how BIG his heart is (towards working for God). He enjoys helping others when in need without looking for anything in return. The next day was a Wednesday, my sister started bedside physical therapy and sat up in bed for the 1st time in 2 months! A week later, she was given a tracheotomy, but off the life support ventilation machine!!! After 3 months in total, inside the hospital bed, my sister came home without the tracheotomy, able to walk, talk in her regular voice and in her right mind! God is an AWESOME God! I thank Apostle Gregory for his passion to spread God's love from his heart and his great leadership to guide and teach us how to love and grow closer to the Lord!
>
> ~ Ms. Delicia Mayes R.T. (R)(MR)

How not to turn back when reached a point of expecting for momentum?

Sometimes it is easy to reach a certain milestone, but it may be equally difficult to stay there, and maintain a certain status quo. It may be equally hard to reach and stay at that point when there is the expectation of the momentum. I say this because just expecting is difficult, there are questions that get asked, questions like, 'when is it really going to happen?' Or, 'what if I am doing it the wrong way?' Or 'is there even a God in Heaven to answer my prayers?' These are all questions that people may ask at the point of weakness and may invite serious doubt about how God can build a great movement of momentum in us. When this happens, there are always ways that one can use in order to get there, and stay there, expecting more from God.

1. Be expectant, it helps you stay awake and ready to run the race when there is a call to, it even helps you to identify the call to do things in the house of God, because many do not even see when there is one.

2. Know what you went through in the past to get you there, it helps you appreciate your past victories, and that God can help you even do more in the future.

3. Understand where you want to see yourself in the future. This will help you keep the focus going because you are fixed at one goal that you always see, no matter what noises get thrown at you. BY understanding where you want to see yourself in the future, you will as well give yourself reason to say you are strong when you are weak, because you know you are courageous enough to not rest until you get to the point where you want to.

4. Always see the finish line (too close to the finish line to turn back). This is vision, you will know exactly the outcome of your actions today (exactly the way it will be in the end), and you are always happy to keep things going the same way, because you are in expectation of something of a great reward, in this case momentum.

5. Declare that the season is right now. This is more to speaking to your body to get ready and stay ready. This is more in line with what we spoke about – telling your body that you are strong when it is weak, because when in expectation of the momentum, you have a strong spirit that encourages the body to stay awake to the race.

CHAPTER **3**

The Movement of Momentum

> **Testimonial**
>
> I have had the opportunity to fellowship with Apostle McCurry over several years in various venues. He has proven to be a true Man-of-God each time we interacted and discussed the vicissitudes of life and religion. Moreover, he is always candid and factual in his conversations with me while expressing truth, based upon experiences displayed throughout his life. Finally, I respect his intellectual prowess as we have talked about theological technicalities regarding the Scriptures and how they impact one's soul salvation. Cheers Apostle Greg McCurry and much success on your road to becoming a very successful author.
>
> ~ Dr. Jonathan J. Pullin
> Founding Principal
> Essie Mae Kiser Foxx Charter School

Something that moves may, or may not make a sound. There is no always one way for people to feel that something is making a movement, therefore, whether we hear it or not, it does not matter, what matters is what sort of results are we going to see coming out of the life that is you.

God says you will know about me, and this is just the sound of great confidence that comes from someone, to the effect that there will indeed be some results to witness. Again, this has nothing to do with the sound that you produce when working towards those same results. In this case, allow me to say that all the sounds, or lack of it, that you may make when making your moves towards just anything my turn out to be just some noise, because in the end, we want to know exactly what you have produced and if we can enjoy the same.

Having said the above, I have been channelling this conversation to that part where I mention that in life, people come in different forms, shapes and abilities. One is able to ride a bicycle so well, the other cannot, and so forth. To the one that is able to ride a bicycle, they can minister in the House of the Lord when there is need to deliver say some charity goods to kids in the rural areas where there is no access to proper road infrastructure. To the one that cannot, they can simply act in the background and make sure that there is the food and groceries to be delivered by donating cash. Between the two of them, they have ministered towards the same cause but only through different means.

Now, in the previous paragraph, I did mention that some can make their marks whilst in the background. This now helps us point again to the fact that making a move does not necessarily mean that you all will be making some noise. The person that rides the bicycle makes some noise, rattles the leaves when stepping on it, but the one that donates money can simply make a wire transfer silently whilst in their bed, and most of the times only the church accountant knows.

You indeed do not have to seek any opportunity to be making noise about what you do for the Kingdom of God, but you have to be worried about what kind of results that you are producing for God.

I keep on mentioning results because when there is a movement of momentum, there is something that will be happening all the way. There is no momentum that moves without producing something at every stage of the way.

Unproductive Christians just move, directionless, and thus make nothing in the end. The provision of direction with which to move in must not be a huge issue, because we do have the word of the Lord to provide us with that.

There is also the issue around believers who want to make sure that they make noise in only in the presence of the pastor, or other congregants, but as soon as they go back home, they are back to their default settings, where they do all sort of anti-Christian things. Yet this race is a continuous one, it never ends, it must follow you everywhere that you go, at home to work, to the train station, to the mall and so forth. This is the reason why I have already mentioned that the movement of the momentum is indeed a continuous process that should be characterised by as much results that get produced along the way.

As an Apostle, and a leader of a church, I can confidently say that I am out here to make a mark whilst still on this Earth. This cannot be the job of my wife to do so, nor is it the job of my uncle, my cousin, my dad or anyone for that matter, you have to make a decision that you want to make a difference in life and make a follow through by yourself.

If you are to sit down, feel sorry for yourself and fold your arms, your mark will only be written in Heaven but will never manifest itself here on Earth for God's people to benefit out of.

> Hebrews 11:1 / NIV /
> *Now faith is confidence in what we hope for and assurance about what we do not see.*

Reading from above, we come across the word 'faith' once again. It says that it is confidence in what we hope for, and assurance about things that people cannot see. This faith, is the one that will act as the starting point to you going on to claim your portion, to confirm the blessing from God. The blessing, combined with the faith in you will maintain a strong movement in you, so much so that you will run and not tire during the entire race.

What is confidence?

This is not some motivation book where I would like to dwell much on the term confidence in that respect. It is a Christian book and I would like to dwell as much as I can on spiritual matters, and thus will define this, and other terms for that matter, in slightly different ways from that which you might hear from a motivational speaker.

Well, when Paul writes about the confidence in what we

hope for in the book of Hebrews, he puts a different angle to how we know the word by throwing in the phrase 'what we hope for'. Therefore, this is not just a matter of self-confidence, but confidence that has nothing to do wit self, rather the confidence that has everything to do with what you want, or wish for things to be like in the future.

The art of life is that of receiving and giving. Others hope to give in future, like I want to be the biggest donor, say in Miami, but others also want to receive certain blessings as life progresses, like I want to have the biggest boat on the shores of New York City. These are all some of the things, or examples of the things that we may wish for.

Speaking of all the above, faith, according to Hebrews 11 verse 1, involves the confidence that when I hope, I will receive what I have been hoping for, and when I wish, I will receive what I have been wishing for.

Moving on, this kind of confidence also is different from the one that we are taught at motivational classes in the sense that it speaks of the connection to a higher power that will be able to deliver exactly what we have been hoping for.

This is the confidence in God, first, because He hears what I have been wishing for through my prayers, and second, that He will be able to deliver exactly, or even more of what I have been hoping for. Therefore, by faith, you are not just being confident in yourself being able to work hard, till the land and produce a couple of metric tons of some crops, but this is being confident in God and His system of working with His people.

After saying the above, I am now going to ask you a question: Are you really confident that God can build (also helped by your faith) enough movement of momentum in you that can last you a lifetime?

Life is always continuous, the reason why you need constant supply of the movement of momentum, believe you can get it, and be confident that the One that makes life happen will also make it happen for you.

***

Testimonial

I've had many stellar moments with Apostle Greg. Every time we met or had a phone conversation, Apostle Greg would give me "food for thought"; nuggets that I can use to stay encouraged. Keep in mind, I do not attend his church, but belong to another. In 2017 I had an opportunity to join Apostle Greg and his wife in Hawaii for their 10th anniversary. Because of this encounter, my life has never been the same. While in Hawaii, Apostle Greg gave me an assignment to listen to his then recent sermon called, "A place called there". Discerning that I was not in the place where God wanted me to be, he began to encourage me in my situation. In my mind I was doing what I thought was right or what I was supposed to do as a Christian woman. I did not realize that fear and tradition was keeping me from moving to the beat that God had destined for my life. I listened to the sermon taking notes along the way; documenting those nuggets that were applicable to me personally. In 2018 I began to make discussions based on those nuggets that have helped me gain momentum – a series of little wins throughout 2018 to help get to my place called "there". I moved from a place where I was stuck and complacent for years; like the man at the pool of Bethesda. I had much peace when I walked away from a marriage and a job that made me feel bound and lacked joy. Apostle Greg's sermon encouraged me to trust God and move when God tells me to. As I move, I grow and get closer to my place called "there". As I get closer to my place, I grow in my ministry, become a better steward over my money, and position myself to be a conduit for Christ to move in the lives of others. I want to say thank you Apostle Greg for taking time to minister and tend to someone else's flock, your direction guided me to MY PLACE CALLED "THERE!"

– Elder Kimberly Moss PhD.

What is an assurance?

Faith has also been said to be an assurance of the things that we currently do not see, at all [Hebrews 11:1(b)].

But what really is this? I always want to start with the online English dictionary so that we start with everyone in the same state of mind as we go. According to this one, there are two definitions of an assurance:

It is a positive declaration intended to give confidence; a promise, and;

It is confidence or certainty in one's own abilities.

We got two really interesting definitions that show two different sides to it, and just like we did with the definition of confidence, we have a two-way definition 'moment' again.

I know I am sounding more like a school teacher now, but that's OK because I am a teacher of the word of God! Well, back to the definitions of the word confidence as used in our Hebrews 11:1 scripture, we will begin with the second definition, which is something that you may hear more from the circular world than in the church of God. This second definition speaks of confidence in a person, or just in oneself, as in doing things the right way and producing perfect results in the end of a what you would have ben doing. This therefore means that there is no other part that is involved, you are just an individual who believes that can do something with utmost perfection, like you are roller-skating with assurance, as an example.

Moving to the *first* definition, it delights me to note that this is something that a Christian would use as defining the word confidence as it was used in Hebrews 11:1. This first definition speaks of confidence as being that confidence that you may have towards the outcome of a process, or things that involve another part. It is like when one is told that someone is coming to fix their broken geyser and they just rise up and tell their kid to wait on taking a bath with cold water, because very soon, someone would have fixed the geyser.

Now faith, belief in God and the benefits of being in Christ, such as developing a great momentum towards life are all anchored in Christ. Nothing is done outside Jesus, therefore, when you say you have confidence as a Christian, you will be saying that you believe that Jesus is going to fix your life, and meet you at your every point of need. You also have confidence that as promised in the scriptures, Jesus will indeed provide an everlasting light unto your life.

> **John 1:3-4 / KJV /**
> *3 All things were made by him; and without him, was not anything was made that was made. 4 In him was life; and the life was the light of men*

When you are confident in something, you can easily relax and have a nice time, knowing that someone is working all day long, just to make sure that you are OK, and got everything that you need. A relaxed and stress-free life (attained through Christ) makes it possible for you to stay alert and catch the movement of the momentum, together with other believers. I always emphasise on the part of doing it together with the body of Christ because when all is said and done, the body of Christ ought to be seen growing, and for that to happen, it needs all hands on deck, which also does underscore the importance around everyone catching, and building on the momentum that we seek to in this year.

***

Now, because you are folding your hands and doing nothing, you are like the ones that are stealing potential gains from the people of God. We also want to see your gift, we also want to be blessed by your gift, your family, your church, your country is still waiting for you to reveal your gift from God!

If you just fold your hands and do nothing at all, chances are nothing will also materialise on your side. God creates an enabling environment that we can make use of for the many blessings we wish for, but He does not carry things and place them before us, just like that! We are the ones that are responsible for making it happen.

Just as I am, I can draw the movement of the momentum to my side, and so can you.

I am one hundred percent responsible for awakening the movement of momentum in me, and so are you.

I am the one that holds the key to the doors that lead to the room where great momentum is, and so do you.

I am one hundred percent responsible for attaining, and maintaining the movement of momentum in me, and so are you.

Therefore, in light of the theme for our church this year, we all carry the same burden, which is to awaken that which was dormant in us; to plant the seed of that which was totally missing in us; to cultivate, and feed that which is already available; and to finish the year together, in support of what we have agreed upon. This will take some strength and dedication, but we are soldiers in Christ, hence shall tire not!

Here are some key verses to read on about how God makes His promises sometimes to His children, He firsts makes them do something, and then the blessing follows, meaning He wants us to be responsible and to be working at all the times. I am sorry, but dormant and stagnant brothers and sisters will find it hard to get testimonies on a daily basis while others do.

> **Genesis 12:1-2 / KJV /**
> *1 Now the Lord had said unto Abram, get thee out of thy country, and from thy kindred, and from thy father's house, unto a land that I will shew thee: 2 And I will make of thee a great nation, and I will bless thee, and make thy name great, and thou shalt be a blessing.*

> **Philippians 3:13-17 / KJV /**
> *13 Brethren, I count not myself to have apprehended: but this one thing I do, forgetting those things which are behind, and reaching forth unto those things which are before 14 I press toward the mark for the prize of the high calling*

of God in Christ Jesus. 15 Let us therefore, as many as be perfect, be thus minded: and if in anything ye be otherwise minded, God shall reveal even this unto you. 16 Nevertheless, whereto we have already attained, let us walk by the same rule, let us mind the same thing. 17 Brethren, be followers together of me, and mark them which walk so as ye have us for an ensample.

I picked the verses above because they are proactive, and both mention a part where a believer, or follower of Christ has to be doing something for the sake of either blessings from God or for working for the Kingdom of God. I will write a summary about the above verses before I move on to the next segment.

In Genesis 12:1, God first asks Abram (later called Abraham) to make a move and out of the land of his ancestors into another land that God was going to show him. Now, as soon as God tells him what to do in the first verse, the second one follows where God makes a promise, that He was going to bless Abram exceedingly. Now, looking at this, it clearly shows how God functions, that we are supposed to act, to work towards something, or just to make a move before blessings from Him start to flow our direction. The art of faith really works that way, the reason why the Bible also calls the faith without action (deeds) dead.

James 2:18-26 / NIV /

17 In the same way, faith by itself, if it is not accompanied by action, is dead. 18 But someone will say, "You have faith; I have deeds." Show me your faith without deeds, and I will show you my faith by my deeds. 19 You believe that there is one God. Good! Even the demons believe that—and shudder. 20 You foolish person, do you want evidence that faith without deeds is useless? 21 Was not our father Abraham considered righteous for what he did when he offered his son Isaac on the altar? 22 You see that his faith and his actions were working together, and his faith was made complete by what he did. 23 And the scripture was fulfilled that says, "Abraham believed God, and it was credited to him as righteousness," and he was called God's friend. 24 You see that a person is considered righteous by what they do and not by faith alone. 25 In the same way, was not even Rahab the prostitute considered righteous for what she did when she gave lodging to the spies and sent them off in a different direction? 26 As the body without the spirit is dead, so faith without deeds is dead.

Here, James gives an account of how much he understood faith that is not followed by action to be dead. Abraham believed in God's word, then acted on it and it is only after that when God confirmed His word on Genesis chapter 12 verse 2. You then ought to also make a move so that God's promise on you is fulfilled.

In the same manner, you also ought to make a move so that the movement of momentum flows through you as it will be doing to the rest of the congregation.

I want to now explain a few things also on the scripture that we put down from the book of Philippians chapter 3.

In verse 13, we are reminded of forgetting about the things from our past. This really helps in creating great focus in you, so much so that all you will now be outing your energy on is not how you were hurt in the past, but actually how you want to see yourself getting better in the future. It will not be too hard to create and enjoy the momentum when you are that focussed.

In verse 14, Paul puts down a phrase that says 'I press on towards the mark', underlying the need to take action, since pressing is also n action word. More so, the use of the word 'pressing' depicts a scenario where not all the conditions for working will be good enough to keep your body health and well looked after. Sometimes being a Christian and keeping up to the standard is hard and requires a great sacrifice. Sometimes you ought to tell yourself that no matter what comes my way, I will keep on soldiering on, doing it for the kingdom of God. There is always a reward in the end.

In verse 15, Paul also puts down a phrase that says 'God shall reveal', meaning that He shall reveal the hidden things, reveal His blessings and so forth, to the people that act (press on) towards the work of the kingdom. More so, using the phrase 'shall reveal,' Paul sends us back to our definition of the word 'assurance' that we put down above, where a believer is driven to know that anything promised is going to be done by the rightful time. However, in light of this section of the book, you ought to understand that these things shall only be revealed to those that work for the Kingdom, or rather to those that take action.

Verses 16 and 17 all have also some action words in 'walk' and 'follow'. In Genesis 12:1, Abram is told by God to 'go', which involves walking, and in Philippians 13:17, Paul tells the Philippians to 'follow' him as he has also followed Christ. All these are different scenarios but have something to do with walking! Interesting isn't it? Interesting in the fact that when building momentum, you also start by walking slowly, when the momentum builds, you begin to walk faster, and when the momentum builds to another level, you then start to run! This is the year of momentum, so believers, let us start by walking now, no one is to be left behind.

Nothing Missing

I came into the Lord not a perfect being, but now I was made whole by Him. The first feeling of the movement of momentum should be inside of me, but if there is something missing, then it will be difficult to feel the movement of the momentum. I therefore declare that in me, there is nothing missing, I am perfect, I am not sick, I am not weak, but just strong and ready to build the momentum for my growth in Christ and in my personal life. Every believer should be heard uttering these kinds of words.

Why nothing missing?
a.	We are kingdom people
b.	The Kingdom is the place of Healing
c.	The Kingdom is a place of abundancy
d.	The Kingdom is a place of joy
e.	The Kingdom is a place of love
f.	The Kingdom is a place of excellency

My Turn, My Time, My Season
Power of embracing the power of God and declaring it is just another way to start the movement of momentum in you. It helps build a strong desire in you, that which gives you the urge to start moving together with others.

Your response to God is going to be key on how God responds back to you. God wants you to be responding this year, He wants you to move, He wants you to make a sound towards Him.

Noise makes noise, sound makes movement. Are you making noise or are you making a sound? How is your sound like? Is it Heavenly or not? Where is the movement of your sound directed do? We want the heavens to hear the sound of momentum coming from this place, wherever it may be. God always responds to the calls, and to the sound of His people.

Faith that builds momentum

Faith comes by hearing, and hearing by the word of God [Romans 10:17]. Faith does not come by reading, but comes by hearing. Faith moves by hearing and faith coming by hearing means that hearing the word of God in the first place makes it a strong foundation to start building your movement of momentum. Faith is the movement of the action of what I heard.

Faith is a belief system, the function of what you have heard long enough to start believing in it. So, be careful what you hear, you might as well start believing in destructive things. Our belief system is always summarised well in the verse below:

> **John 3:16 / KJV /**
> *For God so loved the word, that he gave his only begotten Son, that whosoever believeth in him should not perish, but have everlasting life.*

CHAPTER **4**

The Momentum of Faith

> **Testimonial**
>
> I am rejoicing under that leadership of Apostle Gregory and Sr. Pastor Teresa McCurry. Apostle Gregory is a Hands-On Man of God, he is quite involved, and right up there in serving the community. I have been at New Beginnings Ministries for about a year in a half now, since I have joined, I have grown so much in spiritual terms from being taught by him. He helps us a lot, including as many community members and men (and women) that are incarcerated as well, helping them when they get released. I have seen lives changed for the better as well as mine just from being taught under the leadership of Apostle Gregory. Apostle Gregory is open to everyone in the body of Christ, he has a calendar in his office for all member to freely go into his office fill in a slot of a day and time that you would like to have a one on one with him, how awesome is that? I am so Grateful to God for leading me to a Ministry that is a Word preaching and Word doing kind of church.
>
> ~ Sis Annette Worwell

In this chapter, I want to focus on the kind of faith that makes you leave certain places, certain habits and certain routines, just in order to get to the point where God wants you to. Remember that in the previous chapter, we spoke about God instructing Abraham to leave his land and go to another place, and we also spoke of the Philippians being encouraged by Apostle Paul to 'follow' him as he had also been following Christ.

Looking at all these, we ought to remember that sometimes it may take a lot of effort to rise up and start going towards a certain direction whilst leaving everything behind. In summary, it is never going to be easy. Some people have a lot to lose if they will just get up and leave everything behind on just an instruction from God. There are a lot of things that people have built over the years, and these kinds of things are never easy to leave behind.

What then is required for the pain of leaving your life behind to be minimal? Well, there is the word faith, and trusting in God. When you have faith, and believe that God will support your choices for the sake of His Kingdom, then there will be no pain whatsoever to be talking about. It is therefore this kind of faith that we are talking about in this chapter, hoping that it is going to help a great deal in the building up of the momentum that is going to last for a lifetime.

This faith is a matter of finding strength in the Lord, it is a matter of the great belief which we spoke about, that because He enables you to do great things, then you are able to do so well, above what people may be expecting out of your usual self.

> **Philippians 4:12-13 / KJV /**
> *12 I know how to be abased, and I know how to abound: everywhere and in all things, I am instructed both to be full and to be hungry, both to abound and to suffer need. 13 I can do all things through Christ which strengtheneth me.*

Because Christ is in you, you have great belief and are driven by a higher power that enables you to do and become anything you want in life. Again, it is only a matter of believing that it is going to work, and indeed everything will work such that you may also proclaim that you can do all things through Christ who gives you strength.

Why the need for making that proclamation? Well, looking at the above, we understand that we have already mentioned that many at times it is just difficult to be doing the things that you are supposed to be doing, especially for the Kingdom of God where at times it may seem to be taking ages to realise just a single benefit of the works of your faith. Now in order to overcome the challenges that come along these lines, you will need to have extra strength and courage from God, and only then can you make a move towards just anything that you so desire.

> **Testimonial**
>
> I appreciate Apostle Greg because of his determination to dream and live. There was a time in my life when I stopped dreaming, and living was just a daily ritual of existing. Apostle Greg would often tell me to put a demand on the Holy Spirit. Eventually, I learned by watching his walk with the Lord that this required believing (faith) and believing (faith) will move you to plan. I've seen him do incredible things in life; go places that were probably unimaginable to him 20 years ago. He is a walking example of loving, giving and believing (faith). He loved me enough to give me encouragement while believing that in my life, as in his life, all things are possible. Thank you, Apostle Greg for loving, giving and believing.
>
> With much gratitude and love.
> Terrie Sylvester.

Leaving the past behind

Declare with me here, I am serving the past with a notice – last year is gone and dusted, now I am running into this year looking forward to living my life NOW!!!

Leaving the past behind is not always so easy, it takes courage, and above all, it takes a heart that is full of love and care for others, because if you come to think of it, we are living today so that we better the lives of others that we live with. Therefore, even if you think that you know someone who is selfish, always remember that the same person works, gets paid and in the end sends his children to school and feeds his family – somehow, we are all working (or supposed to be) for someone, that is what God wants us to do. But now, we are just after making sure that we build this momentum together as a church so that we produce better results for the Kingdom.

I would like to pursue a certain lesson here, something to do with building momentum for the benefit of everyone, but on a slightly different note.

The momentum of faith is built on the belief that everything that one does will bear results in the end – even helping others.

Who do you live your life for? Do you believe that you can help build momentum for your youth or any church group?

Life is a journey. In certain instances, we move as a group, but other times each man moves and runs for himself. When moving as a group, things are a lot easier, but when alone, it is certainly cold—but not so for the whole journey. When life gets too comfortable, people get excited, they react and celebrate. In celebrating, some lose themselves and must be brought back to the rightful lane.

When it gets cold, people panic, they get faint-hearted and eventually lose the momentum and thus reverting back to the past because the faith to take them ahead will be dead. When this happens, these will need a friend's consistent presence, a helping hand who will provide comfort and direction. Life is like that, there are always things that need to be dealt with. But even if we have things to deal with, we ought to be seen growing, building the momentum from one stage to another, believing in God for the continued strength.

In all this, remember, you do not live life for yourself. The world needs each and every one of us to serve in different ways. That is how great communities are built, using the momentum from every willing participant.

I am not a good story teller, but I do have one. I hear that in some place somewhere in the world, a certain gentleman was walking through a certain street, and I am told he possessed very observant eyes that were angulating from this end to the other. He is the kind of a character who is very curious about why people do what they do, and why they talk to the people they talk to. As he was looking around, he realised that some people took the opportunity to talk to anyone passing by, as if they wanted to befriend them … or something else. It got him wondering.

With the curiosity of an antelope in front of a colourful python, the man got closer and one of them approached him, just the same way he did to the others. He spoke to him without asking his name or where he had come from.

The fact that this guy spoke to this gentleman for more than two minutes without asking his name showed that he was not interested in becoming his friend or helping him in any way, because if he did, he would have asked what his name was, and introduced himself right away.

He did not care about knowing this gentleman at all. This guy was selling something he soon produced from a small bag, hoping that he was going to buy from him, only for him to turn him down. The moment he told him that he had no money to buy his perfume, the selling guy just turned around and went off without saying goodbye.

This story leaves one wondering if most people are the same way and talk to people only because they want something from them. Maybe this is how the world works now? I have heard of things such as 'networking' with the intention of fostering 'business relationships', which leaves out the important part; the actual relationship, which I believe should come first.

Again, I repeat, relationships are a good way of giving a fresh start to a damaged life. They can be a good way of dealing with the past wounds and starting off to build new and positive momentum that could last for a lifetime.

All this is made possible in faith – believing that God can make your vision come to life, and in this case the vision of building new, positive momentum even with a group of people that you live with.

If you take all these things (instinct to serve oneself) and use them as a measure against just a few people around you, maybe you can get some answers to the question at hand—are people really that selfish? The truth is selfish people do exist amongst us, but also good, caring people are there. Now just take a brief break and ask yourself if this 'instinct' has at one point gotten the better of you. Have you ever used unjustified means to grab only one opportunity that was supposed to go to someone else and not you? I always think of my favourite people when I write about such things—politicians! Most of them end up losing elections because they choose to begin their journeys with not enough momentum because they gather weak team members whose fire will not be enough to burn just one bridge that connects them with negative energy.

People tend to think that winning is everything yet the truth of the matter is that you have to get to a winning end legitimately and with some dignity. I am sure that even after you have given someone some money, you would still want that person to respect you not for the money you have given him, but for just who you are.

What matters the most is exactly who you know yourself to be over and above what people think of you. What you do with yourself and the opportunities coming your way determines the kind of names people start calling you. Some are called 'Chicken' because every time they hear a small sound behind them, the first word that comes into their mind is 'RUN!'

We are thus calling for warriors who are willing to build momentum in the year of 2019, do not be a runner, stick around and let's begin this journey with a single step, have enough faith to carry us to the next stage until we build enough momentum to begin running.

Focused on the Goal

> Philippians 3:14-16 / MSG /
>
> *12-14 I'm not saying that I have this all together, that I have it made. But I am well on my way, reaching out for Christ, who has so wondrously reached out for me. Friends, don't get me wrong:*

By no means do I count myself an expert in all of this, but I've got my eye on the goal, where God is beckoning us onward—to Jesus. I'm off and running, and I'm not turning back.

Testimonial

I can remember it as if it was yesterday, I walked through the doors of NBM not realizing that I was truly walking into my new beginning. I had been praying for months, "God lead me to a ministry where I could be nurtured, matured and every hidden gift and talent would be used for the Body of Christ and God's glory." On my first visit, Apostle Greg spoke a word in my life that has forever changed me. Apostle Greg has shown me, through consistent love, word and deed, how to experience God's love. Apostle Greg changes the lives of every person that he meets.

~ Pastor Adreane Russell

Life itself takes a certain route from the day one is born to the day he dies. You see with people nowadays; you cannot be able to exactly tell what they want to do with their lives until a particular age. All this time, as they will be growing up, certain things will be catching their eyes. Of the things that pass through their eyes, some they just ignore, but for some, they wish if they could do them themselves anytime they get a chance.

People tend to admire certain people around them, the respect and fear they command with other people around, say for example that revered politician who most young people wish would grow up and be like him. You may see that someone can easily like that and purpose it in his heart that one day he will also be just as feared as the ones he sees in TV or anywhere else, as long as it is attractive to him. It is an unfortunate world we live in nowadays, where all that matters is how people will see me, and not how I may bring out the best out of me and create a credible legacy.

This is all wrong, or we do it in the wrong way. I have noticed some sort of a misconception happening for some time now, that when you want to be like someone else, you only focus on what that person has already achieved, and not how he ended up getting there.

There is a lot that goes into success than just showing up faces on TV. Like we have mentioned before, it takes processes, right from baby steps to running when the full momentum has been achieved. Life is always like that.

That is the reason why I also what you to believe that you are capable of starting a movement to build enough momentum within yourself, and also spread that to others so that in the end, we have a vibrant church, which leads to us also having vibrant communities that we live in.

I would love to write about the shape called a circle. The Universe is in a spherical shape, which certainly is a solid form of a circle. In the same way, the sun and the moon are also circular in shape. Humans and animals live on the Universe getting the light and warmth from the moon and the sun. We surely continue to receive wonderful ingredients to our lives through these two 'circular' creations.

Why all this circular talk? In order to come up with a circle, there are many small lines that will have to be joined together. My main focus in all this is on the part of 'joining' the small lines together in order to form one big shape. Unity, togetherness.

> **Psalm 133:1-3 / KJV /**
> *1 Behold how good and how pleasant it is for brethren to dwell together in unity! 2 It is like the precious ointment upon the head that ran down upon the beard, even Aaron's beard: that went down to the skirts of his garments; 3 as the dew of Hermon, and as the dew that descended upon the mountains of Zion: for there the Lord commanded the blessing, even life forever more.*

For life to be beautiful, and for there to be the initial momentum building (in a group), there certainly has to be someone you talk to and share life experiences with pure love. There has to be unity around every group of people living or working together.

But to talk of love and unity in the presence of selfishness is just as misleading as it is destructive to humanity. There is indeed a greater need for people to think also about other people. I personally believe that life revolves around love—the love shown by people who selflessly carry themselves around, combining all their efforts just like those small lines forming a circle. If you may, I recommend that you read the whole book of John and understand how Christ underscores the importance of love in life.

If today I am going to teach someone about how he should live his life in a way that is consistent with a good, frictionless life, I would first make sure that the person is well vested in the benefits arising from leading a selfless lifestyle. It is certainly difficult to build a strong family structure working with selfish people.

A community that is made up of weak family structures also grows weaker and weaker which eventually leads to a very weak, unsuccessful nation. It will be very difficult to work with people pulling a single rope into different directions instead of just one. People have to share a same vision at some point and make sure they do everything necessary together so as to achieve that common goal.

In this book, my focus is going to be, or has already been, on momentum building and maintenance throughout, because we want people to grow, to move with speed and stay up at the top. This momentum is for both individuals and groups, because people start off as individuals but still build relationships as life goes on. These same relationships must be able to reflect great momentum as they continue to work out.

> **Testimonial**
>
> I have known Pastor Greg for only a few years now, and I love him as a brother. We took time out of his day when I was in the hospital, he came to see me, prayed with me, and just sowed love for me. His caring heart is of that of Kind David. His saying of, "GOD loves you and so do I and there's nothing you can do about it," always puts a smile on my face no Matter how I feel. Pastor's preaching is more like teaching his flock and the love he shows them is like a parent is to their child. Church services are truly a blessing to me even though I'm not a member of New Beginnings, I am right at home there. Pastor Greg is truly lead (by the Holy Spirit) to teach the word as well as preach the word, and with GOD's leadership, and reading the word, he is forming into what GOD's plan is for him. Those that are around him get the over-flow of the blessing that GOD gives him in obeying GOD'S command to his shepherds.
>
> Warmest regards,
>
> ~ Deacon Willis McNeal

Faith will take me there.

We just finished speaking about maintaining the same love in a group, and to make sure that one lives not only for himself, but also for others. Now, that might be difficult to maintain, because sometimes when the pastor is preaching about igniting the movement of momentum, not everyone catches the fire at the same speed, some people will need time to do so. As someone who would have responded well to the message, you ought to be patient with others so that the group grows together. If it proves to be hard, believe, have faith that God will take you there (because you have faith).

Faith, is therefore the movement that produces movement. When God spoke to Abraham, He said, "Go to another land, and I will bless you there." [Genesis 12:1-2]. But when God speaks to us that we should leave our land (comfort zones), we remain there and still expect Him to bless us in the place which He said we should get out of.

You can win in this battle; the secret is always to start by seeing it in the spiritual realm.

It starts by you seeing it in your heart, believing it and declaring that 'I am leaving 2018 behind, I am heading off for my destiny.' This is how momentum is built. It prepares you to start a great leap forward.

People of faith do not always stand still even if others in the group are doing so, they are always doing something. They believe that there is a place to go, that there are jobs to complete and will always make a move. You ought to move away from just saying, or speaking about faith, but to actually start making moves. God does see those moves and they eventually become the ones that attract Him into your own life, and later on help to influence the group of people that you might be working with.

Struggling to get walking? Here are a few steps to get you moving.

1. Start by making a decision to not stay put [the four lepers – 2 Kings 7:3]

2. Believe that you will get to where you want to, even if there is initially no hope of you getting there

3. Keep on building your faith by getting into territories that God promised you even if there is no hope for results

Not practising your faith is bad for your progress. People usually believe in the things that they have already seen happening, yet faith is the substance of the things we hope for, but do not see [Hebrews 11:1]. When such happens to you (doubt), you ought to run from this thing, and not just walk away from the habit.

Keeping this kind of behaviour constitutes just one of the weights that Hebrews 12:1 encourages us to lay aside.

Every weight is what hinders you from walking with God. From these kinds of weights, you ought to flee away from, for with them it is not easy to start walking, build some momentum and start running. They just keep you heavy and unable to partake in God's ministry.

2 Timothy 2 verse 22 encourages us to flee from all these things and follow charity, righteousness etc., but more interestingly, it mentions the need for us to also follow FAITH.

The Sequence of Leaving; Walking; Running

I have written before about Abraham being told to leave his then current place of residence so that God blesses him in another land. We then read about walking, and now we just concluded on running. There are indeed lessons to be learnt from this sequence.

Before looking at each of them, I want you to understand one thing, that importantly, this sequence largely resembles someone who is building momentum from the start until the time he or she ends up running.

> Leaving – building momentum
> Walking – some momentum
> Running – full momentum

All these done in faith, after believing the instructive word from God.

Kingdom people make moves

There is a difference between making (a move) and making moves. People in the Kingdom make moves because one move does not produce momentum, but many moves do. When God called on Abraham to leave his place of dwelling it was because he had just made one move which actually was not going to produce enough momentum. God said come out, let us make moves in order to produce enough blessings.

Don't make a move and dwell there, make moves.

An arrow in the air has so much momentum, it has already made moves, and will not stop unless it does at its intended target. Make it a purpose of your heart to never stop moving until the target is reached. And, you can only do this with enough momentum in you.

FAITH it until you make it

Whatever God tells you to do, do it by faith [Hebrews 11:7] [Genesis 6:22].

No one sees the results during the process. You got to have faith, and see them in spirit before everyone else does.

When God tells you to stop, people will see the results.

They will start seeing your house

They will start seeing your children

They will start seeing your cars

They will start seeing your job

They will start seeing you healed, etc.

God will make results come to you, even from a process that no one really understood what was going on.

Read on [Genesis 6:13-22; Genesis 7:1-24]

Testimonial

Thank you for being my Apostle - you may expect those words, but I use them to show my deep appreciation of your work. I'm glad God called you to be a shepherd -there's something supernatural about an Apostle and a congregation being connected at the heart. That's what you demonstrate at New Beginning Ministries.

You also demonstrate Godly Faith - I have grown so much under your teaching, I've learned about the principals of giving, but most of all, that "Love" is the key. You are a down to earth Apostle and that makes your light shine so bright, we, your congregation, do see the God we serve in you.

Well, I love you and there's nothing you can do about it!

Love, Evangelist in Training

Rosetta Gloster

CHAPTER **5**

The Sound Of The Momentum

This message, I did deliver in the month of November of 2018, and it is the day that I introduced the theme of the year 2019 to the congregation: The year of Momentum.

Delivering the message, we spoke about the trail that we had moved on coming to the day when the message was delivered, for in everything, there is the history that builds towards a certain platform, which is the then upcoming 2019. We spoke of the year 2018, and thus the number '18', (taken for the year 2018).

This is the number of life in its fullest, I mean guaranteed and abundant life. I believe we got life now, and we are now obliged to take it ahead and start making moves. We spoke of how sound moves, and we want this same sound of the momentum to be moving, non-stop. We got the life in abundancy, let us make the sound in its complete form as well, so that our quest to build great momentum in this year will not end in a very disappointing end.

The sound of momentum is supposed to be heard somewhere in the middle of a process that would have begun some time back, like we spoke about how we walk, run, and then run faster according to the amount of momentum that we would have built in us.

This reminds me of the story of Elijah the prophet and Ahab, when there was first the process of seeking for the rain, then came the sound of the abundant rain before the rain itself fell.

> 1 Kings 18:41-46 / KJV /
> *41 And said unto Ahab, get thee up, eat and drink; for there is a sound of the abundance of rain. 42 So Ahab went up to eat and drink. And Elijah went up to the top of Carmel and he cast himself down upon the earth, and put his face between his knees. 43 And said to his servant, go up now, look toward the sea, and he went up, and looked, and said, there is nothing. And he said, go again seven times. 44 And it came to pass at the seventh time, that he said, behold, there ariseth a little cloud out of the sea, like a man's hand. And he said, go up, say unto Ahab, prepare thy chariot, and get thee down, that the rain stop thee not. 45 And it came to pass in the meanwhile, that he heaven was black with clouds and wind, and there was a great rain. And Ahab rode and went to Jezreel. 46 And the hand of the Lord was on Elijah, and he girded up his loins, and ran before Ahab to the entrance of Jezreel.*

The story of Elijah that we just read speaks of a quick process where Elijah first hears the sound of the momentum (rain) and tells Ahab to prepare food and celebrate, which he did. What followed was the same Elijah going on top of the mount Carmel and started to pray for the rain. When he was praying, he asked his servant to go and look for clouds towards the sea and it happened for seven times before the cloud was finally seen.

***

> **Testimonial**
>
> I appreciate the spirit of excellence in love that Apostle Gregory McCurry and NBM have always demonstrated to myself and the family. Whether sharing a meal, a message, or memories; the scripture: John13:35, "By this shall all men know that ye are my disciple, if you love one another," has adorned this ministry. I have watched Apostle Greg minister to those who have been incarcerated, and he never fails to share his own life story as the evidence of a changed life through the love and gospel of Jesus Christ. Finally, his ability to love and laugh at himself, while filling others with joy and laughter is a gift from God.
>
> God bless nephew,
>
> ~ Evangelist Mattie Daniels-McNeal

The fact that the servant kept on checking meant that Elijah was expectant of a miracle from God, and secondly, it meant that there is need for people to work, and put in some hours or miles in order for the results of what they have been asking for from God to be finally seen.

The sound of momentum was followed by quick action (the rain) even before everyone was able to go back to their houses for shelter. God speaks and moves so fast that if you fail to hear the sound of the momentum together with others, you might as well get lost in your thoughts as others make moves and enjoy the joys of the Kingdom of God.

I have written a lot about momentum and I fell like I should also input something that has a thing to do with failure.

I looked into life and what I have noticed is that indeed promises are there, from family set-ups to the believers in a Christian set-up. Among all these, know that God's intention is to bless us with as many spiritual blessings, but, as many of us fail to hit the mark as things always go wrong.

It brings me to a point where I ask, do things really go wrong in life? Do we set-up, prepare and make all sorts of arrangements for building momentum only for everything else to end up in an unwanted and disastrous state?

I want you to read on below and try and understand as many things that result in people failing to hear the sound of momentum and completely losing out on what they were intended to benefit on.

As interesting as it may seem to be, life is on its own is another tough adventure by which you will always come across different and new experiences all the times. In the midst of all the events taking place around an individual, not everything may be welcomed or be enjoyed as it happens. I believe that all of us can, in different ways, get into some serious situations by which our own intelligence and tolerance levels will be highly tested. Some of these things just happen without firing any warning shots, in an instant, you can just find yourself deeply rooted in some kind of trouble! It therefore goes down to the way you are able to completely understand and take control of everything taking place around you.

In the Bible we learn about time and chance happening to everyone and everything. The question now would be what actually did you do with your own chance when it came to pass? With some, it is impossible to simply point out to an opportunity as it avails itself. Most people still cannot tell the difference between mere life events and their actual opportunities to go places.

Alright, questions may be ringing in your mind as to why are we speaking of such things in such a year themed around building momentum?

Well, the answer is simple; all the things you do today will one day catch up with you and cause serious changes to your life, whether good or bad, it does not matter except for something will happen under your watch and at a point where you will no longer be able to do much to change things – because in every step that you take, you are building the momentum that will carry you to the next step. So, if you realise a good opportunity today, grab it with haste, never mind about those immediate gains, work hard and be patient enough to see what tomorrow will hold for you!

It does not matter even if you receive the gains of a well taken opportunity after several years, what is of importance are the kind of things following you right now.

Still on the kind of things following right behind you, make sure you choose well what you lay your hands on today, speak of deals, partnerships, relationships and business adventures. If you are holding bad things up in your arms, never dream of you getting the rightful things of this life in the future, unless you repent or change direction today! Our biggest challenge in this generation is that we do not refer to the good things of this life as the things that really matter, we just get carried away by small talk and things that do not get us far.

I call that an illusion of some sort. That is really not the truth about living life to the fullest! When a nation is speaking of a good great people, it should be heard speaking of real things, the things that must have a clearly visible and tangible impact to the nation. Why on earth should you brag about the things that would not even benefit your own neighbour? You should know this thing, that there is actually no achievement that is outside caring for the next person—spread your wings and make sure that the whole world gets the feel of your own achievements!!

Truly speaking, the nature in which we live is in a way such that no one can claim to fully comprehend things. No one is in a position to counter all the things that may come along his way long before things happen. We simply do not have that ability to foresee things long before they happen to us, but the wise always make full use of the past and present events in determining how things might turn out to be in future. All that comes from the need to prepare for life, not just having to live your life going wherever the wind blows! On the back of this, it is also good to know that all of us, whether wise or not, rich or poor, will always have somewhere where we come short, or stumble. Never mind about stumbling anywhere, because no one is perfect, you should instead be worried about what costs would the way you would have stumbled get you into, especially if you find yourself constantly missing the step!

It can be at times funny somehow, how things go wrong for many people, so many colleagues have never taken their time in absorbing and getting to reflect on all that which they do. A decision that is just taken on impulse without proper considerations will always pose some greater difficulties for all those involved, there will not be a certain, and enjoyable future out of such things or style of decision making. My encouragement to all my colleagues out there has always been for them to be smart whenever planning for their diverse activities. It is quite a shameful thing that most of us do not plan for just anything we do.

Being led by a leader who does not plan for his organisation is just like being led by a blind person and still believe he would get you to the rightful destination! The same holds for an individual's life; if you do not plan for your everyday activities, expect a stunted and not normal growth in your general wellbeing. Doing things this way may take us five years just to start building the momentum that we require to start walking before we even speak of running!

So, it can really be easy just for things to go the wrong way in your life if you choose not to do the rightful things. Some people have put up arguments on the issue of the necessary resources needed to get started in any program they would be interested in. They argue that the reason they would have stopped doing some things to develop their lives is because they lacked resources. Alright, the most important thing here is that you make sure that you are rightfully positioned and never just get shifted away by anything that comes against you. Surely God always rewards all those who patiently wait upon Him, times may differ, but everyone will have his own time to be rewarded, you just do not have to be constantly changing positions—keep yourself positioned at the mark, with eyes on the price and all will be well with you!

Testimonial

Apostle McCurry has continued to surpass my expectations for a true friend, and an inspirer. He consistently exemplifies "love in action" by support and encouragement. I can remember when some things were not working for a planned event, venues fell through but Apostle continuously stated it will come together and encouraged us to stay focused. At one event, and during the night of the event, characterized with much hustle and running around, Apostle walked in and said, "I told you he could pull this together." More than the event coming together, we needed someone who actually believes in us and supported us. Thanks for being happy for us.

~ Bishop Charles & Pastor Carmen Dorsey

I have always said to myself that everyone deserves a chance, and rightfully has one at some point. We all grow up differently, get exposed to different things and ways of living at different times. Thus, for some, the way to getting to the top becomes much easier, yet for others, it will always be a mission to get just one thing done. But after all, we all have our own unique ways to life! If you have not found yours, know that it is still out there somewhere just waiting for you to find it, because if you do not, life will remain the same forever, sadly. So, stop complaining about someone who is making it in life and get started in finding your own way!

The storms of life will always come from all different angles, making it no excuse at all for someone not to work hard because something will be fighting against them. We get resistance in our everyday lives, but what do we do? Do we just fold our hands and just watch as things unfold? Not at all, we really have to keep on forging ahead. You should indeed learn how to resist some opposing forces that always seek to shift you from moving into the rightful direction.

Swimming against the tide is a skill that one should learn as he moves. Learn new things whilst moving ahead, the rule should always be motion, with a lot of momentum. It is of course you who is supposed to make sure that everything is correctly positioned around you, including yourself, not your pastor, mother, father or a friend. Remember that you are in charge of yourself, others are just there to motivate you, and that they may help you with what you lack in order to take you to where you would love to be. So, everyone contributes, with you having to put in the largest contribution to your own life!

It is quite imperative for all of us to take serious considerations before getting started with something. You should however be wary of a disease that derails most people's progress; that is the disease of taking the whole year deciding whether or not to get started with something. Some people will just lose out on opportunities simply because they would have taken very long considering what options to take. However, getting into action without proper planning will always make you appear as if you are somehow stupid or have a backward way of doing things.

Without planning, you will always lack that focus necessary for you not to drift away from the intended goal. There is therefore this great need to always be conscious of time keeping as you come up with different means to an intended end. Do not rush things, but at the same time, do not take too long to get to motion.

The little children do fascinate me. They actually carry on their lives so peaceful and without worry even if things are not going on well at home. This is simply because they are not given any duties other than just eating whenever they feel hungry. Not that I am completely incapacitating them, these are sweet people that help us with some few things/chores at home, but just that when it comes to major things or even less, what they think of are not solutions, but parents or guardians! These people greatly believe in their parents' ability to solve any problem coming their way! When seeing their parents, they believe they have all they need, the protection, comfort and affection! I would like to believe that every parent is their children's Superman!

I like this kind of attitude, it leaves you without anything to worry of, your mind is always freed from stress!

However, it will always be good if all this kind of trust the little ones have in their parents is shifted to yourself.

If you believe that you are strong and can do anything, then things will always work out and you will be always in control on the things around you.

Content Whatever the Circumstances

> **Philippians 4:13-14 / MSG /**
> *10-14 I'm glad in God, far happier than you would ever guess—happy that you're again showing such strong concern for me. Not that you ever quit praying and thinking about me. You just had no chance to show it. Actually, I don't have a sense of needing anything personally. I've learned by now to be quite content whatever my circumstances. I'm just as happy with little as with much, with much as with little. I've found the recipe for being happy whether full or hungry, hands full or hands empty. Whatever I have, wherever I am, I can make it through anything in the One who makes me who I am. I don't mean that your help didn't mean a lot to me—it did. It was a beautiful thing that you came alongside me in my troubles.*

Through this, you will move away from just doing things to bringing out extraordinary results out of the work of your hands! Good and result-yielding ideas are first conceived in the mind, then backed up by faith power which comes from the extent to which you believe you can get to the end as a winner. Learn to win even before you start contesting, tell yourself every day that you are the next Miss Universe if you are a model; if you are an athlete, tell yourself that you are the next world champion and work hard towards that!

Still on that, do you know of anything that can make you live a peaceful life besides that which we call our little ones' way? "All those who will stay away from a lie are assured of a peaceful, quiet and admired lifestyle." People lie to themselves, to friends, to pastors, workmates, children, spouses and bosses. The reason people lie is only to try and cover up some 'awkward' situations and or previous mistakes. Here comes the problem now, if you cover up something with a lie today, you would have trapped yourself into the world of lies because it is usually another lie that is going to be needed to justify the one that would have preceded it!

And now the whole system goes wrong, somebody will have to pay in the end! Like we always say, make sure not to create 'air bubbles' as you fill up that jar called life with your work, unless if you want to get an unpleasant surprise in the end, right at the time you will be thinking that the jar is fully loaded.

To the person who lies to himself, you are like the one who is imagining to be the owner of a huge farm full of good crops and hopes to collect a good harvest. He hopes that when the time comes, he will be the first to deliver to the King and be the most loved of them all! On the day of presenting the harvest to the King, our 'imaginary' farmer will be found in a very shameful state such that he cannot be able even to reveal his face to the people. You simply cannot make use of something that is non-existent.

It would be much wiser for you to stay away from lying both to yourself and others, instead, treat all people with respect and honour so that you could avoid the shame that is brought in by deceitfully living your life. After doing all this, you will see how good things can turn out to be!

Anywhere, things do go wrong in life, and whether you get up or not depend on how much you compose yourself in face of challenges.

When running in a race, you do not let go of the momentum that you would have already built simply because you have stumbled at some point, you get up, dust yourself and keep on running.

Going back to our little ones' example, we see the issue of being highly dependent on someone being revealed. Whilst it is a good thing always to seek for advice each time you face some tricky situations in life, you have to be much careful not to overdo it. Some people usually end up failing to think for themselves because they would have developed the habit of letting some other people think for themselves! Habits start out small and are natured into becoming behaviour. Do not always try and look for someone to put ideas into your own head, start moving and think on your own when it is necessary, you have to be wise enough to know when and when not to seek for advice. Many people have unknowingly grown to live some other people's lives through these too much and overdone consultations.

Having said that, it is equally important that you understand that no man is an island, I exist because you exist and vice-versa. We need each other as human beings, do not be like those overzealous people who when told what to do run with the extreme version of the idea given, thereby producing unwanted results out of a good, honest process. What I am saying is remember that even though we do not need to depend on some other people telling us what to do, we still need those people to guide us in their fields of expertise, so that we learn and follow behind them with the aim of excelling in the future.

On another note, it would be a good thing if you can find someone righteous to go seek advice from, do not just pick on anyone at random, study people's ways of doing things before fully engaging with them. Know how to pick put the best mentor and not waste a lot of time and energy on cunning people First, a real mentor will not want anything back from you for his advice. A mentor will not want you to live your life the way he wants and will not care take credit for what you do. Being there as a supporting act is different from being the main actor, many mentors do not get that, your job is to provide the support, direction and advice on what the one being mentored has chosen to do, the way he wants it done.

> **Testimonial**
>
> I met Apostle Greg through our wives' friendship. We also became good friends and I've watched him grow as husband. We found that we have lots of things in common. Especially our love for our wives, nice shoes and good weather! Congratulations my friend!
>
> ~ Godfrey Tull

Well, at this stage I would love to cut the long story short, and just give you a summary of how things go wrong in individuals' lives. Things usually go wrong when:

1. The initial stages in getting started with life will not have been done in a proper way, which is simply a false take-off that results in poor initial momentum gathered right at the beginning.

2. The problems associated with your previous underestimation of things around you will now be manifesting themselves. There are people who simply underestimate the challenges ahead and these never seem to get it right in the race called life.

3. The person involved would have associated himself with disorganised people somewhere along the lines, in a case of bad company leading to equally bad results.

4. The person involved would have deceived himself at some point along the way by taking comfort in those seemingly big, but much smaller benefits that everyone usually comes across.

5. The person involved would have wasted a lot of his strength and resources on non-valuable things.

> **Isaiah 55:2 / NIV /**
> *Why spend money on what is not bread, and your labour on what does not satisfy? Listen, listen to me and eat what is good, and your soul will delight in the richest of fare*

The most unfortunate thing about improper use of resources is that one day they will be no more. Do you even take time thinking of what could possibly happen if the things you have today just vanish away? The point here is not that everyone who has something in his hand is definitely going to lose it someday- not at all, but the point is that you should learn to work towards building your own bigger empire from the few things you have. To achieve this, you must develop the art of correctly allocating the resources you have. This has really worked well for some people-effective allocation of your time and resources.

1. One would have failed to correctly manage his relationships and, or associations. Improper association

can be one of the dangerous steps towards the things falling apart, keep that in mind and know well to keep a God-fearing company.

2. At some point in life someone would have failed to stay face to face with reality.

   This is quite a more interesting side of this issue at hand, things may just go wrong in life all because people usually run away from the truth, some even relocate to some places after some events would have happened in their lives. Instead of looking for solutions, they run! Some may ask what is wrong with running away from demanding situations. All good things are built on focus, honesty and transparency! You come across tricky situations in life, do not run away, open up and try to find solutions from the people around. If you have done something shameful, be brave enough to stand anyone criticising you and find strength to keep on moving with your life!

Testimonial

Since I met Apostle Greg over 11 years ago. I have seen nothing but growth in his spiritual freedom. That is evident in the way that his life continues to flourish!

He is more than an Apostle to me. He is also a brother.

~ Janet Tull

***

What do people do if they seem not to be harvesting the exact crop as that which they would have planted in the first place? Do they teach themselves to love it or they throw it away and wait for the next season to start afresh? I have noticed that most of us would not target the next season and gather for themselves the necessary inputs for them to produce the rightful crops. The issue is not in the end result, it is in the process itself; how actually you gather the inputs, prepare the land, plough, plant, cultivate, weed and water! Some people have no discipline to follow through all such processes.

We tend to run away or avoid such tiresome but rewarding processes. They are things likened to weeds in a field full of corn that can retard progress in one's life. These always resurface themselves every now and then, you have to identify them and be able to do away with them continuously. Do not relax after you solve just one problem in life, some will always come in different ways just as they are many kinds of weeds we see in our fields. A weed in simple terms is anything growing where it is not wanted! Hence one is expected to be willing to deal with anything he does not want as part of his life.

People usually do not want to acknowledge that they have failed at some stages in life, nor will they accept defeat. We all go through phases in life, at some stages we win, at some we don't, that is life and how it is. Inasmuch as it is dangerous to have that defeatist kind of attitude, it is also important for you to know that denying the truth that is on ground about yourself can be another big step towards slowing down progress in your life.

Should you allow then that pessimistic mind to grow in you? Not at all! Or should you just say yes again to everything coming your way? Certainly not again! That is when we go back to the issue of wisdom that is necessary to keep you alert such that you will be able to correctly evaluate each and everything coming into your life thereby coming up with proper solutions on how to react in different situations. In this way, you will not have time to entertain anything that will not have anything with you getting the best out of yourself. Remember that not all that seems to be good will bring in good things into your life; some things we just see with a simple, illusive eye!

Before doing things, we tend to think of so many possible outcomes and I bet even taking permutations! Some will at once give conclusions, obviously pointing to the negative side thereby drawing themselves out of the initially planned objective arguing that they will be by so doing preventing themselves into getting in some kind of trouble. This thing has taken away a lot from us in the sense that most people live in lies thinking they are on the rightful path yet they will not be. When the truth usually comes out, because it will, it will be long too late such that securing a better off position will now be a tall order. A few others standing a chance to go back to the rightful position will do it at a slower and painful pace.

Things will surely go wrong of you think you are too smart to face reality. The good thing about the truth is that even if you try to run away from it, it will remain for ages just waiting for you to come to a point where you see it openly. There is nothing on earth that is strong enough to corrupt the truth, we may do all things and justify all our ways, but the truth, what is right and acceptable by God and the generality of men will remain for as long as there is life on Earth.

All the people who live in truth have always enjoyed each and every day of their lives simply because the truth is only there to set us free.

> **John 8:32 / KJV /**
> *And ye shall know the truth, and the truth shall make you free.*

You desire also to live a free life? Then realise this thing that there is a symbiotic relationship between the truth and righteousness. If you are righteous, God and people love you and hence you attract good things to you leading to you living a free, happy life. The righteousness will surely deliver good things to your life all the times. David puts it well in the Bible;

> **Psalms 37:25-26 / KJV /**
> *I was young and now I am old, yet I have never seen the righteous forsaken or their children begging bread. They are always generous and lend freely; their children will be blessed.*

Righteous people are blessed more and have the liberty to lend freely to the ones that lack. That is when we go to the most important thing about life; that you are blessed so that you could also bless others. That is why I always say as long as you have not yet started helping people then you are not yet successful, you just have enough to live an average life! This also emphasises the points that we raised in the previous chapter, that we build momentum in our lives so that we ignite a fire that is big enough to not just keep us warm at night, but everyone else that we associate with.

I am satisfied that we have covered this issue enough, that things really can go wrong in life and you find yourself failing to run and keep up with others.

However, we still look forward to building great momentum this year, now that we know that things can go wrong and how – which will help counter any sort of challenges ahead.

We do not expect to be raising runners, as in people that run away when facing challenges, but we expect to be raising 'runners', in the form of people who when they hear the sound of something happening, they inquire about what is happening very fast, and are keen to also take part in the build-up to great things.

Things indeed go wrong, sometimes because we would have not followed life processes in a good way, or may be because it's life, hence anything is possible, but like we have mentioned, the going wrong of things should not warranty any degree of slacking to the soldiers in Christ, let us run the race and not tire.

How do you know that there is a sound of momentum ringing?

When the sound of the momentum rings, first, it's waiting for you to hear it, and second, it is waiting for you to respond to it. But then, how do you hear that there is a sound of momentum that is sounding?

1. You ought to hear it
2. You have to expect the sound
3. You have to be ready for it
4. You have to be spiritual and believe in God

I believe in the following scriptures:

> **Romans 8:28 / MSG /**
> *26-28 Meanwhile, the moment we get tired in the waiting, God's Spirit is right alongside helping us along. If we don't know how or what to pray, it doesn't matter. He does our praying in and for us, making prayer out of our wordless sighs, our aching groans. He knows us far better than we know ourselves, knows our pregnant condition, and keeps us present before God. That's why we can be so sure that every detail in our lives of love for God is worked into something good.*

Testimonial

In August of 2016, I remember being in search of a Church that I could call "home", because the house of worship that I had recently left, had served its purpose in my Spiritual walk. I was feeling like my spirit was being smothered, suffocated and not having the ability to grow. I appreciate what I learned in that season in my life and the ministry that had evolved inside of me, but I needed more. It was time to move so that I could really develop a deeper relationship with God. I remember saying that I wanted to be a member of a Church that served the people. I wanted to give away things to the less fortunate because that, to me, was the ultimate service. I walked into New Beginnings Ministries for a visit, I remember Matt, Elder Sharon and Elder Denise were at the doors and they greeted me and my daughter Myranda with the biggest hugs and smiles. I felt like a member, not a visitor. During offering, Apostle Greg (Pastor Greg at the time) stopped me and asked me if I have I ever thought about Ministry, before I could respond, he said, "Well, the Lord told me that you will be walking in Ministry."

 The very next day, one of the Elders contacted me and asked me if I enjoyed the service and to come back and visit again. Well, the very next Sunday, we were back and at that time, they were announcing how they had been Blessed with a new building and that they were moving in October to the new place around the corner. During the announcements, they were having a community giveaway and they were asking everyone to come out and help or bring items that they wanted to donate. At that moment, I knew that God had heard me and he granted my desire. I not only donated items, but I stayed to help with the giveaway. I wasn't even a Member yet, I was still "dating" them. *(cont...)*

God continued to speak to me about New Beginnings because during the giveaway, Elder Terri walked by Myranda and me and asked, "Does anybody dance?" we looked at each other and our eyes lit up because we had been part of the dance Ministry at our previous church and we really enjoyed it. We answered her question and she began to tell us how she was looking for others to join the dance ministry with her. I then realized then that the Holy Spirit was all over "those people." After we left that afternoon, we agreed that when the doors of the church opened, we were joining. That very next Sunday, he opened the doors of the Church and we immediately became members and have been there ever since. Apostle Greg, Pastor Teresa and their New Beginnings family have changed my spiritual life tremendously. I have learned what it means to be a true worshipper of God. The Bible says that "you will know them by their fruit" and our church family is the cream of the crop. He teaches us how to Love one another and doesn't tolerate anything less. He teaches us how to give unselfishly and unto the Lord. He leads by example; his life is an example of how true Christians should move about in this life; always in expectation and preparing for the greater. My faith is growing every day and I am learning how to be in expectation of what God has promised for my life. Apostle Greg does not settle for his spiritual sons and daughters to stay stagnate, he expects growth and prosperity for all of us and will encourage that growth any way that he can. All we have to do is say "Yes" to the call, and he reminds us that God will equip you for whatever he asks you to do. I appreciate him so much. He also took Myranda under his wing as a daughter and speaks life into her and disciplines in Love when necessary. I couldn't have asked God to send me to better house. I am proud to have Apostle Greg and Pastor Theresa as my Spiritual parents.

~ Richanda Jackson

CHAPTER 6

Momentum – Something Out Of Nothing

God can do anything, at any time. This is a popular song among believers, yet it means a great deal in revealing how much God is sovereign, and that He can do wonders in a life just when no one is really expecting. Kindly read the Bible verses below:

> **1 Kings 18:43-44 / KJV /**
> *43 And said to his servant, go up now, look toward the sea, and he went up, and looked, and said, there is nothing. And he said, go again seven times. 44 And it came to pass at the seventh time, that he said, behold, there ariseth a little cloud out of the sea, like a man's hand. And he said, go up, say unto Ahab, prepare thy chariot, and get thee down, that the rain stop thee not.*

Here, Elijah was expecting the rain to come, but everyone else knew not, as there were obviously no clouds hanging in the sky. We know this because Elijah asked for his servant to go and be checking if something (a cloud) was appearing anywhere in the sky, towards the sea.

The servant is said to have gone and looked six times until he then saw something at the seventh try. There was nothing at all when he began to check, but something did appear at his seventh checking when God eventually brought rain on them.

Where does momentum get in here? Alright, the servant and Elijah – if you look at them, Elijah was praying – he was building momentum through prayer. On the other hand, his servant was going to check towards the sea – in other words, he was walking up and down the same route, sounded tedious right? But he was also building momentum as we have mentioned before, that we start by walking until we build enough momentum to run.

> **Testimonial**
>
> I am eternally grateful to Apostle Gregory and Pastor Teresa McCurry for the astronomical impact they have in my life. Every time we meet is an encounter that leaves me greater because of their absolute Excellence. They are 5-Star, First Class and Top Shelf all the way. I never leave their presence without being enriched, encouraged and energized for what's next. You CANNOT be around them without being profoundly influenced by their Greatness, and yet they are the epitome of what it means to be humble and integral and the same time. Any time, money, or energy invested in them or any endeavour they host or sponsor will be a life changing event that you will be grateful to have been a part of.
>
> ~ Elder Natasha Williams

Quickly, I want to give another example from the book of Joshua, kindly read the passage taken from the Bible below:

> **Joshua 6:1-20 / NIV /**
> *1 Now the gates of Jericho were securely barred because of the Israelites. No one went out and no one came in. 2 Then the LORD said to Joshua, "See, I have delivered Jericho into your hands, along with its king and its fighting men. 3 March around the city once with all the armed men. Do this for six days. 4 Have seven priests carry trumpets of rams' horns in front of the ark. On the seventh day, march*

around the city seven times, with the priests blowing the trumpets. 5 When you hear them sound a long blast on the trumpets, have the whole army give a loud shout; then the wall of the city will collapse and the army will go up, everyone straight in." 6 So Joshua son of Nun called the priests and said to them, "Take up the ark of the covenant of the LORD and have seven priests carry trumpets in front of it." 7 And he ordered the army, "Advance! March around the city, with an armed guard going ahead of the ark of the LORD." 8 When Joshua had spoken to the people, the seven priests carrying the seven trumpets before the LORD went forward, blowing their trumpets, and the ark of the LORD's covenant followed them. 9 The armed guard marched ahead of the priests who blew the trumpets, and the rear guard followed the ark. All this time the trumpets were sounding. 10 But Joshua had commanded the army, "Do not give a war cry, do not raise your voices, do not say a word until the day I tell you to shout. Then shout!" 11 So he had the ark of the LORD carried around the city, circling it once. Then the army returned to camp and spent the night there. 12 Joshua got up early the next morning and the priests took up the ark of the LORD.

13 The seven priests carrying the seven trumpets went forward, marching before the ark of the LORD and blowing the trumpets. The armed men went ahead of them and the rear guard followed the ark of the LORD, while the trumpets kept sounding. 14 So on the second day they marched around the city once and returned to the camp. They did this for six days. 15 On the seventh day, they got up at daybreak and marched around the city seven times in the same manner, except that on that day they circled the city seven times. 16 The seventh time around, when the priests sounded the trumpet blast, Joshua commanded the army, "Shout! For the LORD has given you the city! 17 The city and all that is in it are to be devoted to the LORD. Only Rahab the prostitute and all who are with her in her house shall be spared, because she hid the spies we sent. 18 But keep away from the devoted things, so that you will not bring about your own destruction by taking any of them. Otherwise you will make the camp of Israel liable to destruction and bring trouble on it. 19 All the silver and gold and the articles of bronze and iron are sacred to the LORD and must go into his treasury." 20 When the trumpets sounded, the army shouted, and at the sound of

> *the trumpet, when the men gave a loud shout, the wall collapsed; so everyone charged straight in, and they took the city.*

In the passage that you just read, Joshua and the Israelites were set to take up the city of Jericho and as usual, this was going to be done through a combat in the battlefield. However, God had His own way of doing things, and this time, only praise worked through the blowing of the trumpets by the priests.

In this case, momentum was built by a group of people, like we have been emphasising in the previous chapters, that doing things together for the sake of the Kingdom of God is something that God is delighted to see. In this case, He allowed Joshua, the Priests and everyone else to go around the city of Jericho seven times, blowing trumpets each day for seven days, until on verse 20 when the walls finally fell down for the Israelites to gain easy access into the city of Jericho.

Looking at the above, we realise that the servant of Elijah also was made to go and check for the clouds seven times until something appeared out of the sky. This means that the number seven is symbolic in the Bible, but also more importantly, it means that building momentum may take you a long time before the results are clearly visible.

When you are required to go around your own version of the wall (challenges) seven times for seven days do not tire too quickly, keep on going and even if things go wrong like we have said in the previous chapter, just keep your eyes set on the goal.

We have indeed learnt that in order to build the momentum you will have to suffer through a number of challenges but the end is always rewarding in God.

Hence God does anything at any time, He is sovereign, but most importantly, He creates something out of nothing for yourself to enjoy.

Momentum, coming to God with nothing but just what you have.

It does no matter that you come from a poor background, or a background that is troubled by jail, drugs, prostitution or any of the worst things that a human being can ever get involved into. God is able to use and start a fruitful journey with anyone.

Remember, when He called Moses, He did ask him what he did have in his hands. And also remember the story of the five loaves and two fish that fed the five thousand? In that time, Jesus could have fed people with mana that God gave to Israelites out of nothing, because He is God, but He chose to use that which was available, so that we understand that it does not matter how small what we have is, even when thinking of the task ahead, but He wants us to always know that from the most despised of all, He is able to do exceedingly great things.

Having said the above, I want you to understand that as we look ahead to the year of momentum, it is not going to be about what you have, or how rich your family is. This is not going to be the time for making comparisons because all that is vanity in the Kingdom of God.

What will matter in this journey is how committed you are going to be, first to getting yourself ready, and then to the work of God here in His house. When you are all set for the best, God will create great things out of you, even if you have nothing to show for it when the process begins.

God is not looking for perfect people to use, but He is looking for people that carry a heart that is willing to do the work for Him, He is looking for people that are committed and will stop at nothing when it comes to building His church, grow in it and produce as many good fruits of the spirit during their lifetime.

Therefore, come with me, find someone to come with as well, because we all want God to create among us great testimonies, because together we will be strong, together we will build great momentum that will change our lives forever.

Testimonial

The stellar service that I have received from Apostle Greg & New Beginning Ministries, over the last year or so has been exemplary! They always go the extra distance, and will do whatever it takes to get the job done. Apostle Greg is a phenomenal leader, and a great father to many. I am very honored to be connected to such as an amazing gift. Apostle is full of wisdom and because of that many lives have been saved and changed!

-Pastor Brian Timberlake

"Without good direction, people lose their way; the more wise counsel you follow, the better your chances." Proverbs 11:14 MSG

CHAPTER 7

To The Great Years Of Momentum Ahead

In conclusion to this book, I want to stir your spirit towards believing in all the things that we have been speaking about in the book. Remember, the trick is in expecting, and as I write to you just now, I am saying expect the great year ahead in as many ways.

Brace yourself, this is going to be a long and hard final chapter, and I want to take you to life itself, because there is no great years ahead without thinking and discussing about life.

Momentum we said is built from the bottom going upwards, slowly, you start moving, until that time when you are finally running. Therefore, I want to take you down to where life begins and then perhaps close it off by showing you how responsible you are for making things happen.

> **Testimonial**
>
> Why I have chosen to elect Apostle Gregory McCurry as my Spiritual Father.
>
> *"And you shall know a tree by the fruit it bears."*
>
> Meeting apostle Gregory McCurry has been a wonderful blessing. You can tell a man by his character; the character of a possible Greg McCurry has been That of an integrities individual. Often times when walking into a new ministry your concerns are to find integrity, character, and transparency. In my opinion the three are key and have proven to be of great importance when it comes to choosing a leader. The three are all represented in Apostle Gregg, and he has proven to be worthy of following/honoring.
>
> It has been approximately 8 months, and the leadership by example of Apostle Gregg McCurry has,
>
> 1. Revitalized me.
> 2. Empowered me.
> 3. Catapulted me.
>
> To a "Momentous Expectation" of my expected end!
>
> The reason why I've chosen to hear the voice of the Lord in accepting Apostle Gregg McCurry is that he is my Spiritual Father!
>
> ~ Pastor Antoine Burts

The cycle of life

We will now take time to understand the cycle of life before we get deeper into the teachings of coaching yourself to a successful life. A life is begun the day two adults meet in the act that produces a child.

The moment a life is made, the word 'responsibility' is immediately thrown into the fray. It will have to be handled whole-heartedly. As this life develops, the word 'control' is also thrown into play. You will now have to do and not do certain things the way anyone else does, for the sake of those depending on you pulling your act together. It all comes with parenting.

Growing up is a process on its own. It is more like counting numbers, you start from zero going all the way to the hundreds, thousands, millions and more! It all makes sense this way. This number line example is just a simple way of showing people that there is always a way of doing things around, be it at work, school, or home, and definitely at God's house.

The greatest challenge we are facing this day is that of a multitude of people who are reluctant to observe 'ways of doing things' at different places. It is indeed like that this day. But if a teacher asks you to write the number line from zero to ten and you write them not in their order, will you get full marks for that? No. In other words, there are always rules around the places we live.

This is like what we have said already, that in order to succeed with proper momentum building, allow yourself to start by walking, when enough momentum is in you, start jogging, when the momentum grows, start running and eventually sprint when it allows you to do so.

This is all about life processes and they ought to be respected, failure to do so will mostly result in a very disappointing end. I always tell people that sometimes life feels like is a trap that just corners you into an unimaginable trap that you just find yourself in when you are all old and cannot do anything about it, just because you would have grown up doing things the wrong way most of your life.

The Rules Of Life

The cycle of life is used, in this context, to describe the processes an individual follows from early stages of life to maturity. But you will see, as we go further, that there are people involved as well. That is when it becomes important to pay attention to the rules of life, because everyone you are going to associate with will come with different things, demands and requirements that you will need to carefully agree or disagree on and still maintain your relationship at very healthy grounds. Remember, after all, that life revolves around relationships.

Keeping healthy relationships with the people you live and work with creates great stability, and flexibility around your life.

Now, making your life a success as a child of God will greatly depend on how good you are at carefully studying, and understanding your surroundings. These surroundings involve the people you live with at every point in time. It may also involve countries at large, especially in this day where most people have left their home countries to go live and work abroad. I say this because each country has its own broad culture. Country cultures may be different as directed to different groups of people, for example tribes and immigrants. You ought to fully understand all these things and act accordingly just to ensure your survival. People who are swift to act on anything happening around them have greater chances of going around different situations.

Your surroundings describe the things you get in touch with in every single day. This becomes your environment-the place from where you derive your needs from. Speaking of your needs, this includes every essential item, from food to friends. Now it becomes very important to carefully put your ear on the ground and listen carefully to how the environment must be handled. You can then start to do things per the best way for you and the environment. This is one important rule about life that ought not to be ignored.

Having said the above, I want you to pause a little, and ask yourself this question, "Who makes up my environment?" You may take as much time in answering the question. What I want you to remember though, is that do not make the mistake many people make, thinking that they only need their family around them and no one else. That 'environment' must include as many people as possible. You will see that every time a child is born, he/she is kept indoors for a certain period before being allowed to go outside. As the child starts going out of the house, you will see that he/she starts to meet up with different people. These people start becoming part of the child's life and the number grows, or the crowd changes with time. The time spent with these people also increases as the person grows.

The environment a person lives in has great influence and can easily drain the energy out of you so much so that running and building momentum will become difficult. Always be careful how you handle this.

Why does the time spent with other people increase as a person grows? The answer is simple, because they will be doing things together.

Now that is where my story is…where you start doing things with people! When I say doing things with people, I mean that which people do to earn a living. I am sure no one works alone, even if you are a sole business owner, you should have customers of your product as well as suppliers of the materials that you need for your business. This all explains relationships.

I have mentioned already how people, especially the young generation, struggle to handle different people around them. They get frustrated easily and lose interest in life changing ideas/processes because of one 'annoying' person they would have met. I am sure young men, among us see this every day and most have also been tempted to quit, or have left a couple of things unfinished because of the same problem. But life still must be lived and it cannot stop, or change course because one person needs it to. If you desire to go South from where you are standing and you see a huge building blocking the way as soon as you turn around, your immediate response must not be of thinking to leave it for another day. You would rather think of the best way to go around that building until you get back to the rightful track!

These are all decisions that a person can make and get something out of every situation. It is all about results. These do matter at every stage in life. I should say that I have seen a number of poor decision makers in my entire life. This gets me worried about how fast, or slow we can develop our own lives,

TO THE GREAT YEARS OF MOMENTUM AHEAD

and those of the people who need our help out there.

For someone to be a good decision maker, he would have grown up around positive influence. This, you must get from home from the earliest stages. I should say most people miss out on this one. The reason they miss out is that most parents have since given their entire lives to work and forgot that the young blood in their homes need to be educated and be prepared for life.

For some parents, they just do not know how to teach their children about life, they think sending them to school is enough. They do this probably because they would have also not been taught about this important subject when they were still young. For those who are lucky, they can get this positive influence from school, with good friends of course, from reading books and from church.

I mentioned the places, or people where one can get help in decision making in the paragraph above. Keeping this in mind will help you decide which one is best, or close enough to you as soon as you decide you need to know more. Depending on where you stand with your life, you must be wary of who, or which platform you want to get help from. You should create a positive balance between the things you want to do and those you are required to do. For example, do not pick out a source of help that is going to take all your time such that you end up skipping school or work and church. The last thing you want is to gain one aspect about life and lose another one which is important to you. You would have indeed multiplied your numbers, but only by ZERO.

I say the above because everything has a contribution into your building of the momentum, give each equal attention.

Testimonial

"The Lifesaver"

In 1912, chocolate manufacturer Clarence Crane (Cleveland, Ohio) invented Life Savers as a "summer candy" that could withstand heat better than chocolate. Since the mints looked like miniature life preservers, he called them Life Savers. When I think really what a life saver is in my own personal definition would be someone who sees the best in you when everyone only sees someone who does not have value and worth and the very worst in you.

When I met Apostle Greg, I WAS A MESS!!! I was in need of a father to reveal the true Father to me with love and compassion. He truly is the epitome of Jeremiah 31:3; "Yea, I have loved thee with an everlasting love: therefore, with lovingkindness have I drawn thee."

That love drew me into the Kingdom to no longer just exist in life, going through the motions of daily drudgery but taught me how to live for Christ and continues to teach and impart in me God's purpose for my life. He restored my relationship to the Father when I thought I had been abandoned to let me know that God would never leave nor forsake me.

If it had not been for a skit that he gladly and willingly said yes to play in, I believe I would have never got to know the spiritual father I so much love and revere today. Mere words cannot express the gratitude I have for Apostle Greg and his spirit of excellence in ministry.

~ Pastor Denise Washington

So, for you to be good at teaching yourself the things you were not taught from home, you ought to have taken in a lot of the positives about life from your circles, choose them well and always make sure they lead you where there is progress.

Something you cannot run away from, and is about life, is that you ought to know everything about how life itself is supposed to be lived. There are no shortcuts. Life must be FULLY understood. Speaking of LIFE, taking out the letter 'F', for "FULLY", will leave you with the word "LIE" instead of LIFE. Do you really want to live a lie? I guess not. Let us get back to the cycle of life and explore what are the pieces that make up the cycle.

Like I have mentioned before, life is started by two parents who bring a child on earth. This is obviously not the first thing. The first point in the long process is courtship. During courtship, two people in a relationship talk about things of life and how they will have to handle certain aspects about being home owners, or leaders in their own home. People come from different backgrounds. They do not have similar lives and their fortunes are certainly not the same. Thus, it becomes important for aspiring home owners to understand who they are, and what they can offer to the lives they will make in future before getting into it.

Heading a family is indeed a daunting task. You must be mentally and financially prepared for it. So as dating couples, decide on your course of action before taking the first steps.

The first steps must be well in line with your agreed plan. This plan of yours should have been designed in line with what you have realised you can offer to your children. You should take this seriously because it will take you more than twenty years of supporting just one child before he/she can start taking care of him/herself financially.

Besides just financial support, your guidance as a parent is very important. Preparing your child mentally helps him/her with being able to live with different people and handle different life situations. I am sure you have come across very sharp and educated people who get fired from their jobs simply because they are difficult to handle. Life takes more than just intelligence, but mostly you have to be a people person, able to work in a group without creating tension. You learn all this from home. In school, they teach you Maths, but at home they should teach you respect and how to be a hard worker.

People see things and react in different ways. They also choose differently. The way people make choices and are willing to move mountains to live with what they choose to have is determined by how strong their mentality is. Mental strength comes with a series of lessons and habits that would have been cultivated in a human being over a period of time. This process mostly involves the parents. As the child grows and starts to crawl, walk, talk and do many other things, the parent has to start teaching him/her certain aspects about life. Children usually grow up to embrace the things they were taught or got used to at a very young age. You cannot wait until he gets arrested for stealing something at University to start teaching him about how bad it is to steal!

Simple things like saying 'thank you' when you give them sweets are very important. They will also learn to respect through other things like just calling their elder sibling 'brother' and not straight name calling! You should make sure your child enjoys bringing you the dust pan when you sweep the floor, that way, they grow up eager to help whenever they can. When they grow up, they will now be helping society on bigger things. Once a habit settles in, it defines one's character and that becomes what the society will get to enjoy, or dislike.

Why then all this talk about the cycle of life and being organised at a very early stage? Well, I really wanted to conclude this book by showing you that there is more that gets into life and just any process about life starts by getting individuals living organised and respectful lives.

I wanted you to understand that if we are to succeed in building momentum as a church, our individual lives must be on point, our levels of discipline must as well be on point because from when we introduced the book, momentum is about motion and when moving, it takes pain. So, only disciplined people that are ready to take pain for the greater good in future will come out tops at the end of the process.

Testimonial

A tribute to Apostle Gregory McCurry Sr.

I met Apostle Gregory when I was going to an AA "meeting" (on which he was one of the founders of Cocaine Anonymous Group We are Family.) Even though he was a founder of the group that was established in 1985, he returned to active substance use. Next time I met with him, he was a resident at the Noble Motel. My marker on the substance use history, for which I was there alongside Apostle Gregory, smacks of poor decisions, desperation, devastations, abandonment, irresponsible behaviours and neglect.

Then the Drift of years happened as is custom in the land of substance use. I met up with him again – this time he was married and highly active in the church. He was always welcoming me and directing me to a place where "a Prayer could get through". He was the catalyst for which I was slain in the Spirit over thirty-five years ago. Then the Drift of time happened. Life would poke it's head in on the two of us. Most recently, it took place walking "the creek" in 2013. He said, "Hey Ms. Lenora," I said, "Is that you Greg?" We attempted to catch up over a decade of LIFE in three minutes of talking in Euclid Creek. What he emphasized is that "I am pastoring a church"

We exchanged contact information and I began calling him talking about my latest endeavor, completing Graduate school. I went to his church that was located on W.73rd Street. I began attending on Tuesday night. I found his wife and members to be warm and compassionate. *(cont...)*

After that, time passed and health challenges appeared. I called Apostle Greg several times. He listened to me. My plan was not to go the doctor for a growth that was in the breast area, instead, I told him that I was going to use only the Word of God. His response to me was, "Are you sure that you have that kind of Faith?" I said "Yes!" He told me that, "Lenora, God is in the medicine." His witness to me about Our God and medicine made me HEAR God tell me to go to the doctor and that He would meet me there." That is the first Powerful impact that he has had on my life. I expressed that I wanted to learn how to talk in tongues. He ushered me to his lovely wife Teresa, and Minister Barbara, who stayed with me until the Holy Ghost presence was manifested in my speaking in tongues. I have witnessed him being the leader of a small and powerful congregation. The impact of love has drawn me back over five years, and consistently, I seek his guidance and wisdom via him or the Bible study on Tuesday evenings. I am glad to see how he is being used from a Pastor, to an Apostle, The growth in his life is far reaching. I am glad to be a witness and a participant of New Beginning Ministry that definitely has fertile soil. He calls me an "overcomer". I receive It. Words have Power. Each year the church's theme is fuel for the upcoming year.

I am pleased to know that God has redeemed Apostle Gregory from a self-destructive life to bringing WORD to others.

Sincerely,
~ Lenora Flecher

THE END

List of appendices

Appendix 1: Biblical Sources
https://www.biblestudytools.com/niv/
https://www.biblegateway.com
https://www.blueletterbible.org
https://www.gotquestions.org

Appendix 2: Bible versions used
New King James Bible (NKJV)
The Message Bible (MSG)
New International Version (NIV)

About the Author

Apostle Gregory McCurry

Apostle Gregory McCurry is the founder and Apostle of New Beginning Ministries, a Cleveland-based church.

He longs to see lives transformed by introducing "A Real God, To Real People With Real Issues."

Apostle Greg is ordained and faithfully submitted under the leadership of Chief-Apostle Leon D. Nelson Jr. of Embassy Ministries International. He has been preaching and teaching the good news of Jesus Christ for over twenty-five years. His motivating messages have reached many, transcending cultural and denominational barriers within the church and beyond.

Apostle Gregory McCurry offers counselling for men and couples. He has a passion to minister to men through a monthly men's meeting, entitled "Men of Impact", in order to help them step up and be the man God has called them to be and serve the people of God.

He ministers with a knowledge born under biblically grounded principles, together with a heavy prophetic anointing. When "hearing from heaven", under his prophetic mantle, lives are changed, captives are set free, and the power of God is imparted as he is used mightily in the realm of the supernatural. This allows him to administer sage advice to both believers and non-believers.

With a home base in Olmsted Falls, Ohio, Apostle Greg is married to Senior Pastor Teresa "Pastor T" McCurry. He has raised seven children and has a host of grandchildren.

Apostle Gregory McCurry is available for speaking engagements, workshops & seminars;

Contact him at:

Contact information
New Beginning Ministries
2060 west 65th Street
Cleveland, Ohio 44102

www.Mynewbeginning.org
Phone: 216.916.9270 ext. 4
Email: Info@MynewBeginning.org

Follow us: FB- New Beginning Ministries
Tw- @NewBMinistries
IG- newbeginningministries_08

LETONYA F. MOORE
BRAND PROTECTION PRACTITIONER

LeTonya F. Moore, JD is an attorney-entrepreneur with almost twenty years of experience building and helping build successful enterprises. She is the visionary behind 360° Brand Protection Strategies™, developed to address the holistic needs of the entrepreneur. The 360° methodology enables brands to develop strategic growth and expansion to the national, international, and global marketplace. Recently, LeTonya reached a major milestone of introducing her brand protection methodology to the United Kingdom in 2018. She is the founding member of The Global Growth Group (G3), a society of experts collaborating to provide entrepreneurs, including speakers, authors, and coaches with a guided pathway to global protecting their brand both in the US and abroad. Through her work, she is now affectionately known as the Global Brand Protector ™

LeTonya is a sought after speaker who brings value and shares priceless insight and wisdom with her audiences. LeTonya is no stranger to overcoming obstacles and living life on purpose, with purpose. She shares her success story in her, "LeTonya Speaks" motivational presentations that spread a message of faith, perseverance, and the hard work to audiences small and large. LeTonya's "Real Talk" presentation style proves enlightening, educational, and entertaining for diverse demographics.

SPEAKING TOPICS
1. BRAND PROTECTION: LOOKING BEYOND PATENTS, TRADEMARKS, & COPYRIGHTS
2. BUILDING A B.A.I.L. TEAM: PROTECTING YOUR $, YOUR BOOKS, YOUR ASSETS, & YOUR LEGACY
3. 6 M's of BRAND PROTECTION: MINDEST, MOTIVATION, MONIKER, MONEY, MARKETING, & MASTERY
4. HOW TO STOP BRAND STEALING THIEVES WITH A BRAND PROTECTION PLAYBOOK
5. THE TRAILBLAZEHER ™: MY JOURNEY FROM TEEN MOM TO GLOBAL BRAND PROTECTOR

To learn more about LeTonya Moore visit her official website at www.letonyamoore.com.
Follow her on Facebook @iprotectyourbrand
Follow her on Twitter/IG/Snapchat/LinkedIn @letonyamoore
Direct Dial: 256-472-2631 Schedule Consult

Inspire Me Inc.
MESSAGES OF DIVINE GUIDANCE AND INSPIRATION

Invest in you!!
HIRE
Teresa
as your Coach,
or Ministry Leadership Trainer

Through her Impact as a community leader &
Sr. Pastor she quickly discovered her ability to inspire others.

- ➔ Beauty Entrepreneurship Coach
- ➔ International Keynote Speaker & Bible Teacher
- ➔ Church Leadership Trainer

CALL TERESA FOR A $30/30-MINUTE "INSPIRATION CONSULTATION"

Teresa S. McCurry
(216) 466-3801
Teresa@inspiremeinc.com | www.inspiremeinc.com

MCCURRY MINISTRIES INTERNATIONAL
PREACH, TEACH & SING GOOD NEWS

New Beginning Ministries Has relocated to

- 2060 West 65th Street Cleveland, Ohio 44102
- 216-916-9270
- Info@MyNewBeginning.org
- www.MyNewBeginning.org

When you're ready for a change...
Try something "NEW"

God Loves You and you are welcome to worship with us anytime!

Senior Pastor **Gregory** and Pastor **Teresa McCurry**

"We long to see lives transformed by introducing a Real God, to Real People, with Real Issues".

New Beginning Ministries

The Agent-Owned Cloud Brokerage®

Let Pamela help you make your realty dreams a reality!

*Buying   *Selling   *First-Time Buyer   *Investor   *Relocation   *Career

Pamela is a licensed REALTOR® in the Commonwealth of Virginia

Not in Virginia? No Problem

We're in all fifty states; I can connect you with an agent who services your area. Call me, visit my website, or like me on Face Book.

Interested in a career in real estate? To explore a career with Exp Realty Go to:

http://pamelawestbrook.exprealty.careers/

Pamela Westbrook

Broker/**REALTOR®**

(866) 825-7169 Ext. 456

Email: Pamela.westbrook@exprealty.com

Website: pamelawestbrook.exprealty.com

Facebook—www.facebook.com/pwestbrookrealestate

EQUAL HOUSING OPPORTUNITY

REALTOR

www.ingramcontent.com/pod-product-compliance
Lightning Source LLC
Chambersburg PA
CBHW030900170426
43193CB00009BA/691